"A deep, inspiring, inclusive study of th͏ includes all his poems with a beautifu͏ historical analysis by Tanahashi. The r͏ both translators experienced and share in creating this book about the wild her͏ mit poet. Just read a few of these ancient poems and you'll want to take off for the mountains and open your arms to all of life, including the pain and suffering. Read more and you will find your own true heart right here in the present. This book should be read by everyone."

NATALIE GOLDBERG, author of *The Great Spring* and *Writing Down the Bones*

"This comprehensive work of original scholarship and incisively translated verses expands our knowledge of an iconic poet. Here is the Hanshan of social fabric and family as well as of monastery and mountain; the poet of parable, rebuke, and opinion as well as of dharma and icy stream. A sharp-tongued observer of society's failures describes inequality's effects on the spirit; a rapt solitary shares cliff-edge mind with tigers, free-drifting boats, and clouds. Kaz Tanahashi's and Peter Levitt's *The Complete Cold Mountain* joins the shelf of indispensable translations, confirming and extending Hanshan's abiding relevance, presence, history, and range."

JANE HIRSHFIELD, author of *The Beauty* and *Ten Windows: How Great Poems Transform the World*

"Hanshan may be legendary or he may have been three people, but these poems, wherever they came from, are more real than real. They are living Tao and Chan artifacts, well over one thousand years old, brought to life and framed in the most amazing ways with the deepest appreciation for and direct transmission of their down-to-earth, embodied, nondual, poetic elegance and existential poignancy by Kaz Tanahashi and Peter Levitt. This work—the poems themselves coupled with the authors' probing commentaries about their puzzling origins, structure, and essence—is a jewel, with the wondrous property that you can live inside it and let it live inside you for a long, long time."

JON KABAT-ZINN, author of *Full Catastrophe Living* and *Meditation Is Not What You Think*

"*The Complete Cold Mountain* is an extraordinary collection of the complete works of Hanshan; brilliantly translated by Kazuaki Tanahashi and Peter Levitt, it lifts the spirit in the great mountains and beyond."

JOAN HALIFAX, abbot of Upaya Zen Center and author of *Standing at the Edge*

The Complete
COLD MOUNTAIN

Poems of the Legendary Hermit Hanshan

Translated by KAZUAKI TANAHASHI *and* PETER LEVITT

SHAMBHALA Boulder · 2018

Shambhala Publications, Inc.
4720 Walnut Street
Boulder, Colorado 80301
www.shambhala.com

9 8 7 6 5 4 3 2 1

FIRST EDITION
Printed in the United States of America

♾ This edition is printed on acid-free paper that meets the
American National Standards Institute z39.48 Standard.
♻ This book is printed on 30% postconsumer recycled paper.
For more information please visit www.shambhala.com.

Distributed in the United States by Penguin Random House, Inc.,
and in Canada by Penguin Random House Canada Ltd.

ISBN 9781611804263 (paperback)
Library of Congress Cataloging-in-Publication Data Control Number: LCCN 2017045772
LC record available at https://lccn.loc.gov/2017045772

To our beloved sons

KO HANSHAN HESS TANAHASHI *and* TAI LEVITT

Contents

THE COMPLETE COLD MOUNTAIN

Introduction

Peter Levitt

In a most beautiful poem, where pines sway in the wind and bamboo
stalks rustle beneath a moon that rises above the solitary magnificence
of Tiantai Peak, the legendary hermit poet Hanshan ("Cold Mountain"),
who had left behind what he called "the dusty world" of delusion to live
a life of wandering and solitude among the mountains he loved, makes
a confession I find quite moving:

> Scanning the green slopes below,
> I discuss the profound principle with the white cloud.
> Though the feeling of the wild is in mountains and waters,
> truly, I long for a companion of the way.

His statement, like so many others in his extant body of work, is as
characteristically unguarded, wise, and tender as it is true, and not for the
poet alone. My sense is that all people long for a true companion as we
move through the switchback twists and turns of our given lives, climbing
the literal and figurative mountains we come upon or descending into
some of life's more treacherous or mysterious valleys. On occasion, we
might even find ourselves saying, as Hanshan does,

> Lost now on my path,
> Shadow, tell me, which way should I go?

Sometimes we may have the good fortune to meet that companion in
the comings and goings of our daily life, and at other times we may meet
that person, who seems to know us in ways we have always longed to be

known, through the lines of a poem. Though the poems in this collection were written more than twelve hundred years ago, poetry that expresses our common human experience with the unflinching wisdom and truth found in Hanshan's writing has a way of collapsing time and distance, and even cultural differences, because it speaks from the deeply understood heart of life itself.

Because of the compassionate discernment, profound tranquility, unexpected insight, and the occasional outrageous humor of his poetry, Kaz Tanahashi and I have gratefully considered Hanshan one of life's treasured companions for fifty years. As a result of the kinship we feel with him, we gathered together, translated, and now offer readers the most complete version of the poet's work to date in the English language. And, I must say at the outset, as we worked with a great and joyous dedication to enter the original spirit and meaning of each poem, while remaining as faithful as possible to Hanshan's choice of language, we discovered that the poet who had traveled with and within us for so many years had a depth and diversity of expression far greater than even the Hanshan legend and lore portrays or than we had imagined before undertaking the serious task of translation.

There appear to be no accurate, official records that document the life of the poet who took the name Hanshan to express both the place that he lived (in the Tiantai mountain range of southern China) and the nature of his heart and mind. It was the poet's way of saying, *Who I am and where I am and what I am are just one thing.* I do believe, however, that the open, straightforward speech of Hanshan's poems meaningfully serves as a reliable biographical source of this poet who spent decades in virtual solitude in his mountain retreat and yet showed the care he still felt for his fellow human beings by offering to guide them, through the poems he was given to make, in various and sometimes unpredictable and provocative ways.

But, there is more. Kaz has done an extensive study of the poet's life and legend (found on page 217 of this book) and, based on a textual study of the poems, has developed a well-grounded theory that he refers to as the "three Hanshan poets theory." According to Kaz's considerable research into reliable sources, the poet traditionally called Hanshan may actually have been at least three people who wrote under the same name. In part, this theory is based on the time span when the Hanshan poems were written, which is likely more than two hundred years. In addition, there are the poetic and linguistic patterns and historical references found in the poems. These three elements taken together provide convincing evidence for our theory. I encourage you to read Kaz's fascinating chapter called "A Study of the Poet" to find out more.

Based on this groundbreaking discovery, we have organized our book into three parts that highlight the time periods when we believe the poems were written. Nonetheless, because of the consistency of heart and mind found in the poems, I have chosen to speak of Hanshan as just one person. Perhaps it is the shared quality of mind that the collective Hanshan poets possess that allows me to speak in this way. After all, the poems also speak to the Hanshan in us as readers, and so this Hanshan heart and mind do not even belong solely to the writers of these poems.

The act of translation is mysterious to most people, sometimes even to translators themselves. So that we might translate Hanshan as faithfully as possible, Kaz and I dedicated ourselves to following a process that might be considered a modest kind of alchemy. We knew that in order to bring Hanshan's poems across as wholly as possible to readers, we would have to meet this hard-to-find hermit poet not only in the Chinese ideographs in which he wrote his poems, which gave us great pleasure to read, but in that place before the poems were written, the source that caused him to write in the first place—namely, what he experienced in his body, heart, and mind.

To accomplish this subtle and difficult task, we would have to do our best to make the journey to Cold Mountain, as he did, so that we might have as genuine a grasp as possible of Hanshan's life. Perhaps it might be considered the kind of transmission, or intuitive knowing, that many poets and artists in all media speak about receiving from the things of the world just as they are:

> You ask the way to Cold Mountain,
> but the road does not go through.
> In summer, the ice is not yet melted,
> the morning sun remains hidden in mist.
> How can you get here, like I did?
> Our minds are not the same.
> When your mind becomes like mine,
> you will get here, too.

As you can see, to bring Hanshan's poems to readers, we could not simply translate Chinese ideographs into what might be considered their equivalent English words; true translation does not come about in that way. Our journey to Cold Mountain, then, asked us to travel with great respect and care through the ideographs, almost as a lifeline, to that most intimate place from which the words came out: the place that exists outside of language, including the ineffable realms of feelings, perceptions, physical sensations, and moments such as the one that caused Hanshan to end another one of his poems:

> With a bed made of thin grass
> and the blue sky for my cover,
> I rest my head happily on a stone pillow
> and follow the changes of heaven and earth.

Without setting out to make such a journey to that inmost place, how else could we ask our words to convey the nature of Hanshan's direct experience and understanding so that our readers might know his world in a way that is as vivid and alive in their own bodies and minds as it was in his? This was our endeavor, and it was a humbling journey to be sure.

The Hanshan we met "before words" was not just the idealized, eccentric, wild-man hermit living in the mountains, speaking in a manner that was insensible to most people, as has often been described in the Hanshan lore, though certainly the poems make clear that he must have been some of what the legend portrays. But, as the poem and excerpts I've quoted above reveal, and as you will see throughout this collection, he was also a man of deep human and humane feeling, and a person of yearning. He was someone with an insightful societal concern and critique, as well as a devoted spiritual seeker, meditator, and Zen practitioner. And overall, as a lover of the natural world, he was a poet who retreated to the mountains from a society he found extremely disheartening so that, in the fertile quiet of his mountain cave and the surrounding environment of this abode, he might come to experience and know the true nature of life itself.

Indeed, his choice to live "like a lone flying crane," where he would sometimes find himself "grasping [his] knees against a howling wind" or, conversely, find that his life of joyous rambling was "just so good" did not preclude him from experiencing all of the other emotions and states of mind that, in part, reveal the inner truths of what a human life is.

Many of the poems alternately express an almost impossible-to-imagine tranquility as he spends his time "pure and relaxed . . . free from the stain of worldly things . . . mind serene as a white lotus," but there are also poems that express anger or condemn selfishness, greed, and willful ignorance, in a voice that at one moment may be scathing and in the next exposes a genuine wish to help people avoid the hellish results of living in such a way.

In addition, some of Hanshan's poems reveal a profound sense of loss due to the unavoidable truth of impermanence and death as he remembers family and friends from the years before he went off into the mountains, where he had to face his solitary shadow on the wall of his cave. As he expresses it, "before I knew it, two threads of tears came streaming down." But we also hear him expressing periods of true clarity, discernment, and, one might even venture to say, enlightenment, where he experiences his daily life as one of extraordinary peace and joy, lazily playing his lute, reading Laozi or other ancients beneath a tree, or just wandering in the mountains as "a person of nondoing."

And then there is the great compassion and tenderness the poet feels for all living beings. In these poems, Hanshan makes it clear that though we may choose to leave the world behind, a departure that is a fantasy many people entertain from time to time, we should not be surprised that the world finds a way to pack itself among our few belongings. We might even write, as Hanshan did, "Who would think I could leave the dusty world, / just charging up Cold Mountain from the south?"

Some poems reveal his insight into human ignorance and voice the compassion he felt for those who suffer, as when he wonders about a scene he came upon that touched him deeply:

> Rich people meet at a tall building
> decorated with shining lamps.
> When a woman without even a candle
> wants to draw near,
> they quickly push her away,
> back into the shadows.
> How does adding someone diminish the light?
> I wonder, can't they spare it?

Elsewhere, he reaches out through his poetry to encourage others to honor their own nature:

> If you look for it, you can't see it,
> it goes in and out without a gate.
> If you shrink it, it exists in one square inch.
> If you stretch it, it is everywhere.
> If you don't trust and treasure it,
> you cannot encounter it.

Throughout, it is clear that the world of Hanshan, who "chose to live in obscurity, / [his] home beyond the noise and dust of the world," is large; one might even say that it is all-inclusive.

By honoring his own nature and moving to Cold Mountain, Hanshan found a way to live that allowed him to put an end to what he called "useless mixed-up thinking," so that everything could be at rest, and he could live his life as he felt it was meant to be lived, saying:

> In idleness, I write my poems on stone walls,
> accepting whatever happens like an untied boat.

As he went about his daily life, he gathered roots and vegetables in the wild, sometimes wandered twisting paths deep in the mountains to visit venerable monks or friends; he offered medicine to those who might be ill and wrote his poems to track the movement of his mind. And many times he would meditate in his cave through the night or simply sit on the precipice of a cliff, which led him to understand

> my mind is like a solitary cloud, completely free.
> Vast and unhindered, why would I search for worldly things?

It was a realization he was to have again and again, one that inspired his most deeply held desire that all people and all forms of life would also know the freedom of living.

Notes to the Reader

Presentation of the Poems

We present the Hanshan poems in three parts: original poems, early additions, and later additions. This grouping is based on presumptions from the study of rhyming by Edwin G. Pulleyblank and the identified time span of terms and themes found in some of the poems. Please see the last three sections of "A Study of the Poet" (pages 235–43) for details.

Chinese Texts

Following our translation of each poem, we include its original Chinese in unabridged ideographs. This allows the reader to check with the original characters even without the knowledge of any East Asian language. To do so, activate the Chinese language function on your smartphone or computer. Then, with the use of Trackpad Handwriting or TouchPad Handwriting, draw the symbol on your screen or touchpad to find the digital type of the ideograph you are looking for. You can then find detailed information about the character in one of the many online dictionaries.

You can purchase a Chinese learning app (such as Pleco) for your smartphone or tablet and use "Optical Character Recognition" to allow the camera to read the character. You can also use "Full-Screen Handwriting" to draw the ideograph and find the digital form of it within the app.

Chinese Pronunciation

In the following list, the right column gives the approximate English pronunciation of unusual letters used in the corresponding pinyin system found in the left column:

c: ts   q: ch
x: sh   zh: j

Japanese

Macrons are omitted.

Seasons

In ancient East Asia, the lunar calendar was used. The first to third months correspond to spring, and the other seasons follow in three-month periods. The fifteenth day of the month is the day of the full moon.

Notes

Poems with endnotes are marked with an asterisk (*) preceding the poem's number.

Conversion of Poem Numbers

Abbreviation:

H   translation by Robert G. Henricks
RP translation by Red Pine

Conversion from our poem numbers to RP and H numbers is presented on pages 247–50. Conversion from H poem numbers to earlier translations can be found in Robert G. Henricks, *The Poetry of Han-Shan* (Albany: SUNY Press), 424.

PART ONE

ORIGINAL POEMS

Circa Late Sixth to Early Seventh Century

1

You ask the way to Cold Mountain,
but the road does not go through.
In summer, the ice is not yet melted,
the morning sun remains hidden in mist.
How can you get here, like I did?
Our minds are not the same.
When your mind becomes like mine,
you will get here, too.

人間寒山道　寒山路不通　夏天冰未釋　日出霧朦朧
似我何由屆　與君心不同　君心若似我　還得到其中

2

No matter how high you climb Cold Mountain road,
the way to Cold Mountain never ends.
The long valley is stacked with boulders,
its shoreline wet with lush grass.
Slippery moss, regardless of rain,
pine trees singing, even without wind.
Who can go beyond the entangled world
to sit with me in the midst of white clouds?

登陟寒山道　寒山路不窮　谿長石磊磊　澗闊草濛濛
苔滑非關雨　松鳴不假風　誰能超世累　共坐白雲中

13

*3

Amidst cliffs I have made my home.
The paths of birds are beyond human tracing.
What is there beside my garden?
White clouds embracing dark stone.
How many years have I lived in this place,
watching the many changes of winter and spring?
Let me say to those with cauldrons and chimes—
there's no merit in your worthless reputation!

重巖我卜居　鳥道絕人跡　庭際何所有　白雲抱幽石
住茲凡幾年　屢見春冬易　寄語鐘鼎家　虛名定無益

*4

If you want to attain a peaceful life,
settle down at Cold Mountain.
Subtle breezes blow through mysterious pine.
Listen closely, the sound is really good.
Beneath it, someone with graying hair
reads the Yellow Emperor and Laozi without ceasing.
After ten years, I can never return—
I've even forgotten the way I came.

欲得安身處　寒山可長保　微風吹幽松　近聽聲逾好
下有斑白人　喃喃讀黃老　十年歸不得　忘卻來時道

5

Go ahead! Make fun of the way to Cold Mountain,
where there's not a trace of horse or cart.
It's hard to remember valley switchbacks
below layer upon layer of so many peaks.
Dew weeps on a thousand kinds of grasses,
winds sing through the pine.
Lost now on my path,
Shadow, tell me, which way should I go?

可笑寒山道　而無車馬蹤　聯谿難記曲　疊嶂不知重
泣露千般草　吟風一樣松　此時迷徑處　形問影何從

*6

Lute and books should fill your life,
what can fame and money provide?
Abandon your carriage and follow the wisdom of your wife.
A humble cart is pulled by devoted children.
Wind blows over barley drying on the ground,
water floods from the pond stocked with fish.
I often think of wrens
that live peacefully on just one branch.

琴書須自隨　祿位用何為　投輦從賢婦　巾車有孝兒
風吹曝麥地　水溢沃魚池　常念鷦鷯鳥　安身在一枝

7

My mind is like an autumn moon
glowing purely in a clear blue abyss.
Nothing compares to it.
What could I possibly say?

吾心似秋月　碧潭清皎潔　無物堪比倫　教我如何說

8

Once I moved to Cold Mountain, everything was at rest.
No more useless, mixed-up thinking.
In idleness, I write my poems on stone walls,
accepting whatever happens like an untied boat.

一住寒山萬事休　更無雜念掛心頭　閑於石壁題詩句　任運還同不系舟

9

A parrot who lived in the western country
was captured by a net in Wu and brought here.
A beautiful woman plays with it from morning to night,
going in and out of the courtyard of the women's quarters.
She keeps it in a royal golden cage,
with a bar to the door that injured its wing.
Unlike a swan or a crane, it can't
drift with the wind or soar away into the clouds.

鸚鵡宅西國　虞羅捕得歸　美人朝夕弄　出入在庭幃
賜以金籠貯　扃哉損羽衣　不如鴻與鶴　飄颺入雲飛

*10

A city woman with delicate eyebrows
and a white agate-studded sash
teases a parrot surrounded by flowers.
When she plays her lute beneath the moon,
the melody resounds for three months.
Countless people admire her short dance,
but none of this can last.
A lotus cannot withstand the winter cold.

城中娥眉女　珠珮珂珊珊　鸚鵡花前弄　琵琶月下彈
長歌三月響　短舞萬人看　未必長如此　芙蓉不耐寒

11

A handsome young man on a horse
swings his whip and points to the pleasure quarter,
saying, "I will never die."
He has not yet taken a journey.
As the four seasons change, he enjoys flowers,
but one day they all will wither and yellow.
He can't taste the finest cream and honey
until the day he dies.

俊傑馬上郎　揮鞭指柳楊　謂言無死日　終不作梯航
四運花自好　一朝成萎黃　醍醐與石蜜　至死不能嘗

12

In a jeweled hall with hanging pearl screens,
there's a lovely and graceful young woman.
Looking more beautiful than a goddess,
her blossoming figure is like a young peach.
Her house in the east merges with spring mist,
but in her western house, autumn winds rise.
In thirty years, she too will become
like the remains of sugar cane.

玉堂掛珠簾　中有嬋娟子　其貌勝神仙　容華若桃李
東家春霧合　西舍秋風起　更過三十年　還成甘蔗滓

13

Much has been inherited from their parents,
rice and vegetable fields—there's no need to envy others.
The wife rocks the loom, *cr-ack cr-ack.*
The children make baby sounds, *gaa gaa.*
They clap their hands at dancing flowers,
or prop up their chins to listen to bird songs.
Who will come around to appreciate this?
Woodcutters often pass right by.

父母績經多　田園不羨他　婦搖機軋軋　兒弄口啁々
拍手摧花舞　支頤聽鳥歌　誰當來嘆賞　樵客屢經過

*14

I am a woman who lives in Handan.
I sing in low and high pitches.
Happily, in this place where you peacefully hide,
this music has been played for ages.
Already drunk, don't say a word about leaving,
the sun is not yet in the middle of the sky.
In my house, you sleep
beneath a quilt embroidered with silver.

妾在邯鄲住　歌聲亦抑揚　賴我安隱處　此曲舊來長
既醉莫言歸　留連日未央　兒家寢宿處　繡被滿銀床

15

A country person lives in a thatched-roof hut.
In front of his gate, a horse or cart is rarely seen.
Birds gather in the dark forest,
the broad streams teem with fish.
He takes his child to collect nuts and berries,
and together, he and his wife plow the hilly field.
Inside their hut, what do they possess?
Only books on a single shelf.

茅棟野人居　門前車馬疏　林幽偏聚鳥　溪闊本藏魚
山果攜兒摘　皋田共婦鋤　家中何所有　唯有一床書

16

People are a country's foundation,
just like a tree depends on the ground.
If the soil is deep, it supports the spreading branches.
If the soil is poor, the tree will decline.
Do not expose its roots,
or the branches will wither and the fruit will fall.
To get fish by destroying a dam
benefits you just one time.

國以人為本　猶如樹因地　地厚樹扶疏　地薄樹憔悴
不得露其根　枝枯子先墜　決陂以取魚　是取一期利

17

In the third month, when silk worms are small,
women come to pick flowers in a field.
Then they play with butterflies by the fence
and toss toads into the pond.
One gathers plums in her soft sleeves,
another digs up bamboo shoots with a golden hairpin.
If I was forced to compare them,
this village is better than my home.

三月蠶猶小　女人來採花　隈墻弄蝴蝶　臨水擲蝦蟆
羅袖盛梅子　金鎞挑筍芽　鬥論多物色　此地勝餘家

*18

On a legendary horse, with a coral whip,
he dashes down the Luoyang road.
Such a proud, handsome boy
doesn't believe in aging and decline,
though his hair is sure to turn white.
How long can his rosy cheeks remain?
Just look north to the mountain of tombs—
that is the Island of the Immortals.

驪馬珊瑚鞭　驅馳洛陽道　自矜美少年　不信有衰老
白發會應生　紅顏豈長保　但看北邙山　個是蓬萊島

*19

In Luoyang there are many women
who display their charms on a spring day.
They pick roadside blossoms
so each can ornament her topknot.
Their flowery hairdos entice those around,
though others look down on them and glare.
Why seek out troublesome lovers?
Go home to see your husbands.

洛陽多女兒　春日逞華麗　共折路邊花　各持插高髻
髻高花匝匝　人見皆睥睨　別求醶醶憐　將歸見夫婿

20

Girls call to each other while gathering lotus blossoms—
what a lovely pure river village!
They play and play, not noticing the dusk,
or the crazy winds that often come up.
Rising waves lift the ducklings,
large ducks sway in the eddies.
Paddling idly here in a boat,
this vast gentle feeling may never end.

相喚採芙蓉　可憐清江里　游戲不覺暮　屢見狂風起
浪捧鴛鴦兒　波搖鸂鶒子　此時居舟楫　浩蕩情無已

21

In spring, a woman dresses up
to stroll with other women down a southern road.
She enjoys the flowers, but dreads day's turn into night,
and shelters behind a tree, afraid of the blowing wind.
A young man from nearby approaches
on a white horse with a golden bridle.
Why do they dally together so long?
At home, her husband knows.

春女衒容儀　相將南陌陲　看花愁日晚　隱樹怕風吹
年少從傍來　白馬黃金羈　何須久相弄　兒家夫婿知

22

The wife is too lazy to weave at the loom,
the husband too slothful to plow for rice.
He enjoys hunting with his arrows and bow,
while she shuffles around, strumming her lute.
When freezing to the bone, get covered up fast,
to have a full belly, eat some food first.
Who would care about you now
if you suffer and wail to the heavens?

婦女慵經織　男夫懶耨田　輕浮耽挾彈　踮躍拈抹弦
凍骨衣應急　充腸食在先　今誰念於汝　苦痛哭蒼天

When I think back on my young days,
I used to hunt at the imperial field.
Not wanting to be a national envoy,
and saying that being an immortal wasn't good enough,
I'd gallop astride my white horse,
shouting at rabbits and letting my green hawk fly.
Without realizing it, I took a great plunge.
Could anyone see my white hair now and feel pity?

尋思少年日　游獵向平陵　國使職非願　神仙未足稱
聯翩騎白馬　喝兔放蒼鷹　不覺大流落　皤皤誰見矜

24

As a youth, I carried scriptures and a hoe,
while living with my brother's family.
But others made accusations
and even my own wife turned her back.
So I left the dusty world
to live idly, reading books.
Who can offer a bucketful of water
to rescue this fish from its cart track puddle?

少小帶經鋤　本將兄共居　緣遭他輩責　剩被自妻疏
拋絕紅塵境　常游好閱書　誰能借斗水　活取轍中魚

*25

When Dong was young,
he used to visit the imperial palace
in a jacket made of yellow duckling feathers,
so he resembled a painting.
He always rode on a horse with white hooves
that kicked up the red dust.
Onlookers packed the roadside,
wondering whose child he could be.

董郎年少時　出入帝京裏　衫作嫩鵝黃　容儀畫相似
常騎踏雪馬　拂拂紅塵起　觀者滿路傍　個是誰家子

26

Your writing and judgment are not at all poor,
so I wonder why you didn't pass the official exam.
The examiners may have been twisted or perverse
to rinse off your dirt, seeking sores and scars.
This must be your destiny.
Try again this winter.
Even if a blind person shoots at a sparrow's eye,
an accidental hit is not impossible!

書判全非弱　嫌身不得官　銓曹被拗折　洗垢覓瘡瘢
必也關天命　今冬更試看　盲兒射雀目　偶中亦非難

27

In the village where I live,
people flatter me as incomparable.
Yesterday, I went to the city
and was glared at by dogs.
People either hated my narrow pants
or said my jacket was too long.
While the sparrow hawk's eyes are crossed,
sparrows dance with confidence.

我在村中住　衆推無比方　昨日到城下　卻被狗形相
或嫌褲太窄　或說衫少長　攣卻鷂子眼　雀兒舞堂堂

28

Wandering, I arrive at Above the Sky Pavilion,
where I climb the hundred-foot tower in vain.
Even if we nurture life, our lives are short,
how will making myself study turn me into a lord?
It's useless to follow the advice of immature people.
Why should I be ashamed of my white hair?
Not yet as straight as an arrow,
I won't be bent like a hook.

浪造凌霄閣　虛登百尺樓　養生仍夭命　誘讀詎封侯
不用從黃口　何須厭白頭　未能端似箭　且莫曲如鈎

29

Raising girls brings up many fears.
Those already born should be trained well.
Push at their heads to make them attentive,
whip their backs to keep their mouths shut.
If they can't operate a shuttle and loom,
how can they use brooms and dustpans?
Old woman Zhang tells her donkey foal,
"When you grow up, don't be like your mother."

養女畏太多　已生須訓誘　搔頭遣小心　鞭背令緘口
未解乘機杼　那堪事箕箒　張婆語驢駒　汝大不如母

*30

Last spring, when birds were warbling,
I thought of my brothers, young and old.
Now, in autumn, as chrysanthemums decline,
I think of my own birth.
Deep green rivers make me weep,
the dust of battles covers the land.
What a pity! Within a hundred years
the capital city of Xian was destroyed.

去年春鳥鳴　此時思弟兄　今年秋菊爛　此時思發生
綠水千腸咽　黃雲四面平　哀哉百年內　腸斷憶咸京

31

A cuckoo atop a flower
chirps in a lovely voice.
A beautiful woman whose face is like a jewel
looks toward it and strums her harp.
Playing like this is not enough.
We long for love when we are young,
but flowers and birds both fly away.
I shed tears facing the autumn wind.

花上黃鶯子　關關聲可憐　美人顏似玉　對此弄鳴弦
玩之能不足　眷戀在齠年　花飛鳥亦散　灑淚秋風前

32

Young women play at dusk
as the breeze fills the road with fragrance.
With golden butterflies sewn on their skirts,
jeweled duck hairpins adorn them.
Even their maids wear fine red silk,
and their eunuchs dress in purple brocade.
But look! Those who lose the way
become frightened when their hair turns white.

群女戲夕陽　風來滿路香　綴裙金蛺蝶　插髻玉鴛鴦
角婢紅羅縝　閹奴紫錦裳　為觀失道者　鬢白心惶惶

33

A five-colored phoenix
lives in a paulownia, eating bamboo nuts.
It moves slowly with decorum,
there's a peaceful tone in its song.
Why did it come out yesterday?
Perhaps, to spend some time with me.
When it hears my harp and singing,
it dances, rejoicing in the day!

有鳥五色彡　棲桐食竹實　徐動合禮儀　和鳴中音律
昨來何以至　為吾暫時出　儻聞弦歌聲　作舞欣今日

*34

How pleasant! The body of Chaos,
that neither eats rice nor pisses,
met with the one whose pliers and chisel
made the nine holes of a human form.
Since then, people work for clothes and food,
and worry about taxes year after year.
Thousands of people fight for a penny—
battling each other, they scream for their lives.

快哉混沌身　不飯復不尿　遭得誰鑽鑿　因茲立九竅
朝朝為衣食　歲歲愁租調　千個爭一錢　聚頭亡命叫

35

Rich people meet at a tall building
decorated with shining lamps.
When a woman without even a candle
wants to draw near,
they quickly push her away,
back into the shadows.
How does adding someone diminish the light?
I wonder, can't they spare it?

富兒會高堂　華燈何煒煌　此時無燭者　心願處其傍
不意遭排遣　還歸暗處藏　益人明詎損　頓訝惜餘光

*36

Zou's wife, who is modest,
and Du's mother from Handan,
young and old women together,
share the same respectable appearance.
Yesterday they met at a restaurant,
but were rejected and sent to the back of the room
because their skirts were torn.
They had to eat roasted rice cakes others left behind.

氐眼鄒公妻　邯鄲杜生母　二人同老少　一種好面首
昨日會客場　惡衣排在後　只為著破裙　吃他殘餻麨

*37

The Shi family had two children
whose talents served the Qi and Chu courts.
Both mastered literature and the martial arts,
relying on themselves alone to acquire positions.
Mr. Mao asked about their secret, saying,
"I want to train my children in your way,"
but at Qin and Wei, neither was successful.
The timing was off, and the fit was bad.

施家有兩兒　以藝干齊楚　文武各自備　託身為得所
孟公問其術　我子親教汝　秦衛兩不成　失時成齟齬

*38

In general, things have their own use,
with each use being right.
If you miss the proper usage,
things will be lacking here and there.
Trying to put a square peg in a round hole,
sadly, just won't work.
The legendary horse, Hualiu, trying to catch a mouse
isn't even as good as a lame kitten.

夫物有所用　用之各有宜　用之若失所　一缺復一虧
圓鑿而方枘　悲哉空爾為　驊騮將捕鼠　不及跛貓兒

Brothers separated in five counties,
a father and his children from three different regions—
they all want to investigate flying like owls
and discover how White Rabbit swims.
In dreams, they receive sacred melons,
and keep divine tangerines.
How will they ever get home from such a distance,
packed like fish in a stream?

弟兄同五郡　父子本三州　欲驗飛鴞集　須征白兔游
靈瓜夢裏受　神橘座中收　鄉國何迢遞　同魚寄水流

*40

Once, a master calligrapher and swordsman
met three luminous, sacred kings.
He governed the east, but received no praise,
his western offensive gained him no rank.
He studied literature while learning martial arts,
and combined martial arts with his literary study.
Now that he is old,
his remaining years are not worth mentioning.

一為書劍客　三遇聖明君　東守文不賞　西征武不勛
學文兼學武　學武兼學文　今日既老矣　餘生不足云

41

Heaven created a tree one hundred feet tall
that could be cut into long lengths for lumber.
What a pity this wood for a master carpenter
was abandoned in a dark valley.
Its heart remains strong after many years,
but gradually its bark stripped off, leaving it bald.
If there's someone who knows how to use it,
it might make a strong post for a horse-barn.

天生百尺樹　剪作長條木　可惜棟梁材　拋之在幽谷
年多心尚勁　日久皮漸禿　識者取將來　猶堪柱馬屋

*42

Zhuangzi talked about his funeral,
"Make heaven and earth my coffin."
When I depart,
just wrap a reed screen around me.
Death certainly feeds green flies—
don't bring a white crane to take me away.
If I starve on Mount Souyang
as a devoted follower, death will be a pleasure, too.

莊子說送終　天地為棺槨　吾歸此有時　唯須一番箔
死將餧青蠅　弔不勞白鶴　餓著首陽山　生廉死亦樂

43

Astride a galloping horse, I arrive at a ruined city,
where the desolation moves me deeply.
Old high and low parapets,
large or small abandoned tombs—
my mugwort shadow shakes all alone,
I freeze at the sound of the cemetery trees.
How sad the bones of worldly people are!
In the history of the immortals, they bear no name.

驅馬度荒城　荒城動客情　高低舊雉堞　大小古墳塋
自振孤蓬影　長凝拱木聲　所嗟皆俗骨　仙史更無名

*44

The seasons never cease.
Years come and go
and all things are renewed.
The nine heavens are not destroyed,
east glows bright, the west turns dark,
flowers fall and open once again.
Only those in the Yellow Spring
remain in complete darkness, never to return.

四時無止息　年去又年來　萬物有代謝　九天無朽摧
東明又西暗　花落復花開　唯有黃泉客　冥冥去不回

*45

Why are young people unhappy?
They're sad to see old people's white hair.
Why does white hair make them sad?
They worry when they feel the pressure of time.
But if they went to live on the Eastern Mountain of Death,
or were appointed to guard the Northern Cemetery—
I can't bear to say these words.
It would hurt old people to hear them.

少年何所愁　愁見鬢毛白　白更何所愁　愁見日逼迫
移向東岱居　配守北邙宅　何忍出此言　此言傷老客

46

Two turtles riding in an oxcart
that dashes down the street are having fun.
A poisonous scorpion approaches
and begs for a ride.
Not to give it isn't kind,
but as soon as they do, the scorpion kills them both.
I can't even say how fast—a finger snap!
Their kindness is met with a sting!

兩龜乘犢車　驀出路頭戲　一蠆從傍來　苦死欲求寄
不載爽人情　始載被沈累　彈指不可論　行恩卻遭刺

47

An old woman in a house to the east
has been rich for just three to five years.
In the past she was poorer than I,
but laughs now that I have no money.
So, she laughs at me later,
just as I laughed at her before.
Although we don't quit laughing at each other,
east and west are not so far apart.

東家一老婆　富來三五年　昔日貧於我　今笑我無錢
渠笑我在後　我笑渠在前　相笑儻不止　東邊復西邊

48

Rich people have many burdens on their hands,
concerning matters they just won't accept.
A warehouse of poor rice that's turned red,
yet they won't lend it to others who struggle.
Always ready with a trick, when buying thick brocade,
they pick up the damask first.
When their lives are over,
only green flies will mourn.

富兒多鞅掌　觸事難祇承　倉米已赫赤　不貸人斗升
轉懷鉤距意　買絹先揀綾　若至臨終日　吊客有蒼蠅

*49

In the past, I saw a brilliant man
whose broad knowledge and sterling spirit
were beyond compare. Once he passed
the national exam, his name was celebrated everywhere.
His five-ideograph poems surpassed all others,
as an official, his governing excelled even his superiors.
No one could follow in his tracks.
Then, he suddenly turned greedy for wealth, property, and love.
Things crashed down like melting ice, beyond what words can say.

余曾昔睹聰明士　博達英靈無比倫　一選嘉名喧宇宙　五言詩句越諸人
為官治化超先輩　直為無能繼後塵　忽然富貴貪財色　瓦解冰消不可陳

*50

A white crane bore a bitter peach
and flew a thousand miles in one breath.
Wanting to reach the Mountain of Immortals,
he began to consume it,
but before finishing, his feathers fell out—
he dropped out of the flock with a heart full of misery.
Upon returning to his nest, his wife
and children didn't recognize him.

白鶴銜苦桃　千里作一息　欲往蓬萊山　將此充糧食
未達毛摧落　離群心慘惻　卻歸舊來巢　妻子不相識

How glorious is the lady of the Lu family,
always known as "Free of Sorrow."
Greedily, she gathers flowers on horseback,
and loves paddling out to harvest lotuses from a boat.
Kneeling on a green bear seat,
draped in a blue phoenix robe,
how sad that in less than a hundred years
she won't avoid returning to the hill of tombs.

璨璨盧家女　舊來名莫愁　貪乘摘花馬　樂撈採蓮舟
膝坐綠熊席　身披青鳳裘　哀傷百年內　不免歸山丘

52

Who can live forever without dying?
Death comes for everyone.
I used to think he was eight feet tall,
but, all of a sudden, he's a scoop of dust.
The underground world has neither dawn nor day,
though grass is always green in spring.
When I become sad,
a mournful wind in the pines kills me.

誰家長不死　死事舊來均　始憶八尺漢　俄成一聚塵
黃泉無曉日　青草有時春　行到傷心處　松風愁殺人

*53

Like someone who's always drunk,
the years stream by without ceasing.
Concealed behind the mugwort,
how dim the moon is at dawn.
Flesh and bone will completely vanish,
spirit can wither and fade.
If you are bound to get an iron bit in your mouth,
there's no point in reading Laozi.

竟日常如醉　流年不暫停　埋著蓬蒿下　曉月何冥冥
骨肉消散盡　魂魄幾凋零　遮莫咬鐵口　無因讀老經

*54

The hanging willow dark as mist,
flower petals whirling like sleet in the air,
the husband lives far from his wife—
in another province, his wife longs for him.
Each has a life under heaven,
but when will they see each other again?
She writes to a woman beneath a glowing moon,
"Don't keep a swallow nest at your house."

垂柳暗如煙　飛花飄似霰　夫居離婦州　婦住思夫縣
各在天一涯　何時得相見　寄語明月樓　莫貯雙飛燕

55

If you have wine, invite each other for a drink.
If you have meat, share the meal.
You will die sooner or later,
so make an effort while you're young and strong.
A jeweled belt is just a passing glory,
a golden hairpin won't always adorn.
Old man Zhang and old woman Zheng
both departed; not a word about them has arrived.

有酒相招飲　有肉相呼吃　黃泉前後人　少壯須努力
玉帶暫時華　金釵非久飾　張翁與鄭婆　一去無消息

*56

Peach blossoms try to make it through summer,
but wind and moons don't wait.
Look for people from the Han,
not a single one can be found.
Every morning flowers fall,
year after year, people change.
Even this land, where dust scatters like ash,
used to be a great ocean.

桃花欲經夏　風月催不待　訪覓漢時人　能無一個在
朝朝花遷落　歲歲人移改　今日揚塵處　昔時為大海

57

Look at a flower among leaves.
How long will it be appealing?
Today it fears someone will pluck it,
tomorrow it will wait to be swept away.
We should pity those who are seductive,
after some years they will turn old.
Just compare the world to this flower—
how long can youthful beauty last?

君看葉裏花　能得幾時好　今日畏人攀　明朝待誰掃
可憐嬌艷情　年多轉成老　將世比於花　紅顏豈長保

58

I see a hundred or so dogs,
each one with grungy hair.
Some lie down as they like.
Some walk around, if they like.
When they're thrown a bone
they gnaw at each other and fight.
There's just too little bone
for so many to have an equal share.

我見百十狗　個個毛猙獰　臥者渠自臥　行者渠自行
投之一塊骨　相與啀喍爭　良由為骨少　狗多分不平

59

Far in the distance, I see
white clouds spread out in all directions.
Horned owls and crows are well fed and fat,
while the mythical phoenixes starve and wander nearby.
An excellent horse gets sent to the gravel pit,
while a lame donkey is kept at a fine hall.
The heavens are too high for me to question—
cuckoos and wrens fly over the ocean waves.

極目兮長望　白雲四茫茫　鴟鴉飽腰腮　鸞鳳饑徬徨
駿馬放石磧　蹇驢能至堂　天高不可問　鷦鷯在滄浪

60

If you remain silent and don't speak,
what will your descendants say?
If you hide in a forest or bamboo grove,
how will your wisdom shine through?
A withered tree is not protected,
wind and frost cause disease.
If you plow a gravel field with an ox,
how will you ever harvest rice?

默默永無言　後生何所述　隱居在林藪　智日何由出
枯槁非堅衛　風霜成夭疾　土牛耕石田　未有得稻日

*61

Fulfilling means fulfilling the spirit,
this is called being fulfilled.
Transforming means transforming the form,
this is called being transformed.
If we fulfill the spirit and transform the form,
we can reach the stage of an immortal.
Not fulfilling the spirit means no transformation,
no escaping death and suffering in the end.

益者益其精　可名為有益　易者易其形　是名之有易
能益復能易　當得上仙籍　無益復無易　終不免死厄

62

How shallow worldly people are,
though human minds are not the same.
Old man Yin laughs at old man Liu.
Old man Liu laughs at old man Yin.
How come they laugh at each other?
Both of their minds are one-sided.
If you compete, piling up loads on a cart,
the loads will whoosh down on you.

俗薄真成薄　人心個不同　殷翁笑柳老　柳老笑殷翁
何故兩相笑　俱行譏誚中　裝車競嶵嵬　翻載各瀧涷

Gifted people have sharp minds—
they hear something once and understand the wondrous.
Ordinary people have pure minds—
they think thoroughly and speak the essence.
Slow people are ignorant and dull,
with a stubbornness that's hard to crack through.
They wait for blood to drip from their heads
to realize they're injured and could die.
See with your eyes open that a thief
is executed in a crowded marketplace,
his body tossed away like trash.
In that moment, to whom can he plead his case?
A strong man who's been split in half by a sword
has a human face, but an animal mind.
How can we prevent such a thing?

上人心猛利　一聞便知妙　中流心清淨　審思云甚要
下士鈍暗癡　頑皮最難裂　直待血淋頭　始知自摧滅
看取開眼賊　鬧市集人決　死尸棄如塵　此時向誰說
男兒大丈夫　一刀兩段截　人面禽獸心　造作何時歇

*64

How many types of people are there under heaven?
If we talk it over, there are many.
Empress Jiapo had a husband,
Laozi had no wife.
Wei's child was lovely,
Zhong's daughter was extremely ugly.
If the trend keeps going west,
I'm heading east.

天下幾種人　論時色數有　賈婆如許夫　黃老元無婦
衛氏兒可憐　鐘家女極醜　渠若向西行　我便東邊走

65

Wobbly, poor scholars,
hungry and extremely cold,
love to sit alone, composing poems,
squeak squeaking with all their power.
But, who would read such lowly people?
My advice to you is stop sighing.
If you write your poems on rice cakes,
even begging dogs won't eat them.

蹭蹬諸貧士　饑寒成至極　閑居好作詩　札札用心力
賤他言孰採　勸君休嘆息　題安糊餅上　乞狗也不吃

*66

Someone boasts about his practice,
saying he's even better than Lords Zhou and Confucius.
But when looked at closely, he's hardheaded,
with a big lumbering body.
Pulled by a rope, he doesn't progress,
pierced by an awl, he still won't budge.
He's just like ancient Yang's crane—
pitifully dull-witted since birth.

或有衒行人　才藝過周孔　見罷頭兀兀　看時身侗侗
繩牽未肯行　錐刺猶不動　恰似羊公鶴　可憐生甊甊

67

A poor donkey lacks one foot of food,
while a rich dog can leave three inches behind.
If the extra is shared, it's not fair to the poor,
so rich and poor should split the food in half.
But, if the donkey takes more than its fill,
it makes the dog starve right away.
If I think too much about what you should get,
I could get anxious and depressed.

貧驢欠一尺　富狗剩三寸　若分貧不平　中半富與困
始取驢飽足　卻令狗饑頓　為汝熟思量　令我也愁悶

The man called Liu is eighty-two.
The woman, Lan, just eighteen.
Together, husband and wife come to one hundred years,
but their love for each other is crafty and cunning.
Their son, Wutu, toys with a jade ball.
Their daughter, Wanna, flips an earthen spool.
They're like buds that sprout from a decayed willow,
bound to be killed by the goddess of frost.

柳郎八十二　藍嫂一十八　夫妻共百年　相憐情狡獪
弄璋字烏儳　擲瓦名婠妠　屢見枯楊黃　常遭青女殺

69

A wretchedly hungry and frozen man,
clearly born different from animals or fish,
lived a long time beneath a polished stone tomb.
Sometimes he'd weep on the street corner
after dreaming for days about hot, cooked rice.
But he got through winter without even a jacket,
carrying his bundle of thatch
and five scoops of bran.

大有饑寒客　生將獸魚殊　長存磨石下　時哭路邊隅
累日空思飯　經冬不識襦　唯齎一束草　並帶五升麩

70

How brightly lit this wine shop is!
Strong wine,
and a high lovely banner.
They make sure their servings are exact,
so everyone wonders why their wine doesn't sell.
That family keeps many fierce dogs.
When children are sent to buy wine,
the dogs nip and drive them away.

赫赫誰壚肆　其酒甚濃厚　可憐高幡幟　極目平升斗
何意訝不售　其家多猛狗　童子欲來沽　狗咬便是走

*71

If you're rich and noble, those near and far gather around—
it's just that you have so much money and rice.
If you're poor and lowly, even family members go away—
it's not that your siblings are few.
Hurry up, go back to your home,
the pavilion where the wise are invited is not yet open.
Recklessly, you wander Red Sparrow Avenue,
wearing out your leather sandals.

富貴疏親聚　只為多錢米　貧賤骨肉離　非關少兄弟
急須歸去來　招賢閣未啟　浪行朱雀街　踏破皮鞋底

*72

I see a foolish man
who keeps two or three wives
and has raised eight or nine children.
Still, overall, he follows a sensible hand.
His grown children have new households,
though he hasn't passed down his resources.
But he lives like someone who uses
yellow bark for a donkey strap—
soon he will know that bitterness comes later on.

我見一癡漢　仍居三兩婦　養得八九兒　總是隨宜手
丁戶是新差　資財非舊有　黃蘗作驢鞦　始知苦在後

*73

With the new grain not ripe,
and the old grain already gone,
I wanted to borrow a bushel or so.
I stood outside my neighbor's gate, but wavered.
When the husband came out, he had me ask his wife,
when the wife came out, she sent me back to her husband.
Their stinginess will never help those who are starving,
their wealth has made them rich in stupidity.

新穀尚未熟　舊穀今已無　就貸一斗許　門外立踟躕
夫出教問婦　婦出遣問夫　慳惜不救乏　財多為累愚

*74

We can laugh about a lot about things,
so let me mention a few.
Mr. Zhou was wealthy and prospering,
while Maozi was poor and kept getting stuck.
A dwarf entertainer was taken to an excessive meal,
though faithful but starving Fangshuo was not invited.
Many people sing popular songs,
but few can sing the peaceful tune "White Snow."

大有好笑事　略陳三五個　張公富奢華　孟子貧轗軻
只取侏儒飽　不憐方朔餓　巴歌唱者多　白雪無人和

75

An old man marries a young woman,
when his hair turns white, his wife can't stand it.
An old woman marries a young man,
when her complexion yellows, her husband isn't pleased.
An old man marries an old woman,
neither of them rejects the other.
A young woman marries a young man,
together they show their love.

老翁娶少婦　發白婦不耐　老婆嫁少夫　面黃夫不愛
老翁娶老婆　一一無棄背　少婦嫁少夫　兩兩相憐態

76

A good-looking young man
has widely read scriptures and history.
People address him as "master,"
and everyone says he's a scholar.
But he hasn't yet acquired an official position
and doesn't know how to use a plow.
In winter, he goes around in a torn cloth jacket.
Is his scholarship to blame?

雍容美少年　博覽諸經史　盡號曰先生　皆稱為學士
未能得官職　不解秉耒耜　冬披破布衫　蓋是書誤己

*77

A good person shouldn't stay poor.
If you have no money, manage your affairs.
Get and keep a cow
who will give birth to five calves.
These will have more calves
that multiply without end.
Let me offer a word: Lord Tao Zhu's
wealth and yours can be the same.

丈夫莫守困　無錢須經紀　養得一牸牛　生得五犢子
犢子又生兒　積數無窮已　寄語陶朱公　富與君相似

78

Why are you so indecisive?
Make up your mind and settle down.
The south has many diseases,
in the north, winds are bitter and cold.
The wilderness isn't suitable for living—
poisonous river water can't be drunk.
Let your spirit return home,
enjoy the mulberries from my garden.

之子何惶惶　卜居須自審　南方瘴癘多　北地風霜甚
荒陬不可居　毒川難可飲　魂兮歸去來　食我家園葚

*79

In last night's dream I returned home
and saw my wife weaving at the loom.
She rested her shuttle, and seemed lost in thought,
with no strength to lift it again.
When I called, she turned to look,
but didn't recognize me.
So many years have passed—
the color of my hair has changed.

昨夜夢還家　見婦機中織　駐梭如有思　擎梭似無力
呼之回面視　況復不相識　應是別多年　鬢毛非舊色

*80

Humans live barely one hundred years,
but worry weighs you down for a thousand.
As soon as your own illness improves,
you become anxious for your children and grandchildren.
You inspect the root of the rice plant,
and squint at the top of the mulberry.
Only when your counterweight plunges to the bottom
of the eastern sea, will you get to know some rest.

人生不滿百　常懷千載憂　自身病始可　又為子孫愁
下視禾根土　上看桑樹頭　秤錘落東海　到底始知休

81

North of the city, old man Zhong
kept a houseful of wine and meat.
When his wife died,
mourning guests filled his home.
When Zhong himself died,
no one wept for him at all.
Those who had eaten the meat and drunk his wine—
how cold their hearts and stomachs!

城北仲家翁　渠家多酒肉　仲翁婦死時　弔客滿堂屋
仲翁自身亡　能無一人哭　吃他杯饌者　何太冷心腹

As I walked around an ancient burial site,
my tears dried up, but my sighs would not die down.
A tomb had been broken into, crushing the outer box.
The pierced coffin exposed whitened bones
and ash jars leaning at strange angles—
the courtier's hairpin and scepter had been stolen.
When the winds struck, they'd taken over the inside,
scattering dust and ashes all around.

我行經古墳　淚盡嗟存沒　塚破壓黃腸　棺穿露白骨
欹斜有甕瓶　振撥無簪笏　風至攬其中　灰塵亂坲坲

83

Since growing up, I've been disturbed
by the chaos of worldly affairs,
but I can't just abandon ordinary people,
so I visit from time to time.
Yesterday I went to a funeral for the fifth son of Xu.
Today we send off Liu's third child.
There's not a moment of peace
for my sorrowful heart.

出身既擾擾　世事非一狀　未能舍流俗　所以相追訪
昨吊徐五死　今送劉三葬　終日不得閑　為此心悽愴

*84

If there's pleasure, enjoy it—
don't miss the chance!
Although human life is said to last one hundred years,
how will you use up thirty thousand days?
We pass through this world in an instant—
don't argue about money or complain.
The last chapter of the *Book of Filial Piety*
speaks about this in detail.

有樂且須樂　時哉不可失　雖云一百年　豈滿三萬日
寄世是須臾　論錢莫啾唧　孝經末後章　委曲陳情畢

85

I was pretty poor in the past,
but this morning I'm the poorest and freezing.
Whatever I do doesn't go smoothly,
and the paths I travel only lead to trouble.
When I walk on mud, I sprain my leg,
when I sit at a village meeting, it gives me an ulcer.
Having lost my calico cat,
old rats surround my rice jar.

昔時可可貧　今朝最貧凍　作事不諧和　觸途成佗傯
行泥屢腳屈　坐社頻腹痛　失卻斑貓兒　老鼠圍飯甕

86

In the days when I had money,
I always lent you some.
Now you're warm with a full belly,
but you don't share anything with me.
Think about it: your desire to gain
was like my hoping to receive.
Having and not having switch back and forth.
I beg you to turn this over in your mind.

是我有錢日　恆為汝貸將　汝今既飽暖　見我不分張
須憶汝欲得　似我今承望　有無更代事　勸汝熟思量

87

Let me advise you about a few things.
Consider them and you'll know I'm wise.
If you're very poor, go ahead and sell your house.
If you get a bit of wealth, buy a rice field.
When your stomach's empty, you can't run around,
or sleep with your head on a pillow.
So that others can read this advice,
hang it on the eastern wall where the sun first shines.

教汝數般事　思量知我賢　極貧忍賣屋　才富須買田
空腹不得走　枕頭須莫眠　此言期眾見　掛在日東邊

*88

"If others are wise, accept it.
 If they're not wise, don't get together."
"If you are wise, others will accept you.
 If you're not wise, others will reject you."
 If you admire the good, and sympathize with those less able,
 you have a place among compassionate people.
 I encourage you to follow the latter saying of Zizhang,
 and throw away the former words of Zijia.

他賢君即受　不賢君莫與　君賢他見容　不賢他亦拒
嘉善矜不能　仁徒方得所　勸逐子張言　拋卻卜商語

*89

A good-looking man
who had mastered all six arts
went to see the south, but was driven back to the north.
He went to see the west, and was chased toward the east,
so he wandered a long time, drifting like water weed,
and flying about like mugwort without taking a rest.
I ask what kind of thing he is—
his family name is poverty; suffering is his given name.

一人好頭肚　六藝盡皆通　南見驅歸北　西見趁向東
長漂如泛萍　不息似飛蓬　問是何等色　姓貧名曰窮

90

Yesterday, I saw trees beside a river
damaged beyond description,
with two or three left standing
that had countless gouges from an ax.
Frost had withered their sparse leaves,
waves had battered their decaying roots.
Our lives are just like this—
what's the use of holding a grudge against the universe?

昨見河邊樹　摧殘不可論　二三餘干在　千萬斧刀痕
霜凋萎疏葉　波沖枯朽根　生處當如此　何用怨乾坤

*91

"Life and death are destined.
 Wealth and nobility are determined by heaven."
These are the words of an ancient,
I'm not misquoting.
Wise people tend to have a short life,
while fools live long.
Good-for-nothings have great wealth,
awakened ones have none.

死生元有命　富貴本由天　此是古人語　吾今非謬傳
聰明好短命　癡騃卻長年　鈍物豐財寶　醒醒漢無錢

92

Since heaven and earth began,
humans have lived between them.
You get lost, then are spat out into the mist,
you awaken, but are quickly blown about by the wind.
When you are favored, you have wealth and nobility,
when you are robbed, you suffer and are poor.
People are like a bunch of pebbles—
all things are due to the lord of heaven.

二儀既開闢　人乃居其中　迷汝即吐霧　醒汝即吹風
惜汝即富貴　奪汝即貧窮　碌碌群漢子　萬事由天公

*93

Raising a child without a teacher
is worse than keeping a mouse at a roadhouse inn.
How would they ever meet a good person,
or hear what they have to say?
Cloth can be dyed with sweet or stinky grass.
Waste no time choosing friends and companions,
like peddling fresh fish under the scorching sun—
don't let others laugh at you.

養子不經師　不及都亭鼠　何曾見好人　豈聞長者語
為染在薰蕕　應須擇朋侶　五月販鮮魚　莫教人笑汝

94

Several foolish youths
go about their tasks carelessly.
They haven't even read ten books
but stubbornly make editorial corrections.
They got hold of the Confucius chapter on Conduct
and called it a guideline for robbers and thieves.
They're no different from book worms
that gnaw through their covers.

三五癡後生　作事不真實　未讀十卷書　強把雌黃筆
將他儒行篇　喚作賊盜律　脫體似蟫蟲　咬破他書帙

*95

A scholar named Wang
laughed and said my poems have many faults:
"You don't know about hunch back.
You don't understand skinny legs.
These flat and slanted tones don't rhyme,
and there's one cliché after another."
I laughed. "The poems you make
are like a blind person describing the sun."

有個王秀才　笑我詩多失　云不識蜂腰　仍不會鶴膝
平側不解壓　凡言取次出　我笑你作詩　如盲徒詠日

*96

Though he's not truly a hermit,
he calls himself a mountain sage.
He's just an official of Lu who wears a conical silk hat,
but also loves a turban of twining vines.
He says he's as pure as Chaofu and Xuyou,
and would be ashamed to serve Emperor Yao or Shun.
He's like a monkey who puts a fish basket on his head,
mimicking seekers who try to avoid the dusty world.

元非隱逸士　自號山林人　仕魯蒙幘帛　且愛裹練巾
道有巢許操　恥為堯舜臣　獼猴罩帽子　學人避風塵

97

Wise people aren't greedy,
but the ignorant are keen to stoke the furnace.
They take over someone's barley field,
then try to get his entire bamboo grove.
Those of you who shoulder in, seeking riches,
gnashing your teeth, driving your servants and mares,
take a look outside your gate—
tombstones scatter beneath the oaks and pines.

賢士不貪婪　癡人好爐冶　麥地占他家　竹園皆我者
努膊覓錢財　切齒驅奴馬　須看郭門外　壘壘松柏下

*98

I've often heard that Emperor Wu of Han
and Emperor Shi of Qin
favored the arts of sorcery,
but neither extended his life.
Already, Wu's golden terrace has been shattered,
and Shi's town of Shaqiu destroyed.
By now, their mounded tombs in Moulang and Liqiu
are overtaken by weeds.

常聞漢武帝　爰及秦始皇　俱好神仙術　延年竟不長
金臺既摧折　沙丘遂滅亡　茂陵與驪岳　今日草茫茫

99

Greedy people are good at accumulating wealth,
like owls who love their young,
though when the children grow large, they devour their mothers.
Possessions are just like this.
When you give them away, you grow happy,
when you hoard them, it brings misfortune.
Owning nothing causes no harm,
like a bird flapping its wings in the great blue sky.

貪人好聚財　恰如鴞愛子　子大而食母　財多還害己
散之即福生　聚之即禍起　無財亦無禍　鼓翼青雲裏

100

The water of the Yellow River is vast—
it flows eastward without ceasing.
Drifting slowly on, without ever clearing up,
everyone's life comes to an end.
Even if you wish to ride a white cloud,
how can you grow wings?
During the years when your hair is black,
in motion or stillness, give yourself completely.

浩浩黃河水　東流長不息　悠悠不見清　人人壽有極
苟欲乘白雲　曷由生羽翼　唯當鬒髮時　行住須努力

*101

I've wanted to move to East Rock
for so many years.
Yesterday I climbed the ivy-covered path,
but got stopped halfway up by mist and wind.
It was hard to press on, the narrow path grasping my robe,
the moss sticking to my sandals.
For now, I'll stay beneath the cinnamon tree
and sleep with the white cloud as my pillow.

欲向東巖去　於今無量年　昨來攀葛上　半路困風煙
徑窄衣難進　苔粘履不前　住茲丹桂下　且枕白雲眠

Born thirty years ago,
I've wandered thousands of miles—
from rivers that merge with the grasslands
to the frontier where red dust appears.
In vain, I tried herbal medicine and sorcery,
studying books and reciting history out loud.
Today I return to Cold Mountain,
where the stream is my pillow, cleansing my ears.

出生三十年　當游千萬里　行江青草合　入塞紅塵起
煉藥空求仙　讀書兼詠史　今日歸寒山　枕流兼洗耳

103

By divination, I chose my hidden abode.
There's nothing else to say about Tiantai.
Monkeys cry out, the valley mist is cold,
mountain colors lead to my thatched gate.
I twist off pine boughs to cover my room,
and draw valley water to make a pond.
Letting the myriad things come to rest,
I gather bracken to carry me through the year.

卜擇幽居地　天臺更莫言　猿啼谿霧冷　嶽色草門連
折葉覆松室　開池引澗泉　已甘休萬事　採蕨度殘年

104

My home is under the green mossy rock.
The overgrown garden is not weeded out.
New wisteria vines entangle
the upright ancient rugged stones.
Monkeys pluck the wild fruit,
white herons scoop up fish in the pond.
With one or two Daoist books,
I read, mumbling beneath a tree.

家住綠巖下　庭蕪更不芟　新藤垂繚繞　古石豎巉巖
山果獼猴摘　池魚白鷺銜　仙書一兩卷　樹下讀喃喃

105

The white cloud is naturally idle.
I never purchased this mountain.
When climbing down a dangerous path, I use my cane,
when climbing up a steep ravine, I grab a vine.
At the bottom of the valley, pines are always green,
in the nearby gorge, rocks are mottled.
Although friends are cut off,
when spring arrives, birds chirp gently.

自在白雲閑　從來非買山　下危須策杖　上險捉藤攀
澗底松常翠　谿邊石自斑　友朋雖阻絕　春至鳥關關

106

I have only one garment,
not silk, not brocade.
If you ask the color,
it's neither purple nor red.
In summer, it's a jacket,
in winter, it's my quilt.
Winter or summer, it simply changes use.
Year after year, it's been just this way.

我今有一襦　非羅復非綺　借問作何色　不紅亦不紫
夏天將作衫　冬天將作被　冬夏遞互用　長年只這是

*107

How many years have I lived on Cold Mountain?
Alone, I sing with no worries at all.
The woven mugwort door doesn't close, but here it's always serene,
the spring pouring nectar in a constant flow.
On the ground of my cave, medicine in a clay pot boils in the fire pit.
There are jars of yellow pine pollen, cypress bud tea, and fragrant gel.
When I'm hungry, I eat an *agada* pellet.
My heart is well balanced as I lean on top of a stone.

久住寒山凡幾秋　獨吟歌曲絕無憂　蓬扉不掩常幽寂　泉湧甘漿長自流
石室地爐砂鼎沸　松黃柏茗乳香甌　饑餐一粒伽陀藥　心地調和倚石頭

108

With a vast net of stars, the night is bright and deep.
In my cave, I light a single lamp before the moon sets.
Its full radiance is not a polished jade—
hanging in the blue sky, this is my heart.

衆星羅列夜明深　巖點孤燈月未沈　圓滿光華不磨瑩　掛在青天是我心

109

The scroll is crowded with remarkable poems.
A jar overflows with a sage's wine.
When walking, he loves to watch the cow and a kid.
When sitting, he's not separate from left or right.
Frost and dew slip beneath the thatched eaves
as the moon blossom shines in the window
made from the mouth of a jar.
At this time, sipping from two small bottles of wine,
he chants a few of his poems.

滿卷才子詩　溢壺聖人酒　行愛觀牛犢　坐不離左右
霜露入茅簷　月華明甕牖　此時吸兩甌　吟詩三兩首

*110

When fools read my poems,
they don't understand, so they laugh and make fun.
When ordinary people read my poems,
they think and say, "They have a point."
When wise ones read my poems
they grasp them with big full smiles.
It's just like Yangxiu who saw the ideographs "young female,"
and immediately understood "wondrous."

下愚讀我詩　不解卻嗤誚　中庸讀我詩　思量云甚要
上賢讀我詩　把著滿面笑　楊脩見幼婦　一覽便知妙

*111

Five hundred five-character-column verses.
Seventy-nine seven-character-column verses.
Twenty-one three-character-column verses.
The total comes to six hundred poems.
I wrote them all over my rocky cave.
I'm proud to say I'm good at it.
If you can understand my poems,
truly you are Tathagata, the mother!

五言五百篇　七字七十九　三字二十一　都來六百首
一例書巖石　自誇云好手　若能會我詩　真是如來母

112

Retreating to the deep forest,
I've been a country person since birth.
Raised to be natural and straightforward,
I don't flatter when I speak.
I take care of myself and don't think about others' fortunes,
trusting they will get the pearls.
How can I be the same as those who drift on water,
eyeing wild ducks atop the waves?

偃息深林下　從生是農夫　立身既質直　出語無諂諛
保我不鑒璧　信君方得珠　焉能同泛灩　極目波上鳧

113

Do I have a body or not?
Is this a self or not?
I investigate this fully,
sitting for a long time, leaning against a rock.
Green grass starts to grow between my legs.
On top of my head, red dust falls.
Already, when worldly people look at me,
they offer wine and fruit on the platform for my coffin.

有身與無身　是我復非我　如此審思量　遷延倚巖坐
足間青草生　頂上紅塵墮　已見俗中人　靈床施酒果

114

Holding to my aspiration, I won't be rolled around by others.
I know I'm not a mat.
After wandering, I arrived at this mountain forest
where I lay down alone on a rugged rock.
A smooth talker came by and urged me
to quickly take some gold and jewelry.
It's like chiseling a wall to plant mugwort—
such things do no good.

秉志不可卷　須知我匪席　浪造山林中　獨臥盤陀石
辯士來勸餘　速令受金璧　鑿墻植蓬蒿　若此非有益

*115

If Cold Mountain utters these words
no one will believe them.
Honey is sweet for people to enjoy,
but bitter bark keeps them away.
Going along with people's feelings brings pleasure,
opposing their ideas sparks resentment.
Just look at wooden puppets
acting out their tragic scenes.

寒山出此語　此語無人信　蜜甜足人嘗　黃蘗苦難近
順情生喜悅　逆意多瞋恨　但看木傀儡　弄了一場困

116

Wise ones threw me out.
Fools, I hurl you away.
I'm neither foolish nor wise,
so from now on, I'll have nothing to do with you.
Going into night, I sing to the bright moon.
Immersed in dawn, I dance with the white cloud.
How can I rest my mouth and hands,
sitting up straight as my shaggy hair grows?

智者君抛我　愚者我抛君　非愚亦非智　從此斷相聞
入夜歌明月　浸晨舞白雲　焉能住口手　端坐鬢紛紛

*117

There is a mist eater
whose abode is closed to worldly people.
When he speaks, he is stern yet clear,
summer and autumn alike.
Dark mountain streams run bright and pure,
high pines rustle in the chilly winds.
If you sit there for even half a day,
you'll abandon a hundred years of worry.

有一餐霞子　其居諱俗游　論時實蕭爽　在夏亦如秋
幽澗常瀝瀝　高松風颼颼　其中半日坐　忘卻百年愁

Water flows broadly on the plains.
The Hill of Immortals links up with Mount Siming.
The immortals' graceful city is highest
among peaks that rise up like green folding screens.
Far off, the view is endless,
with rugged forces that come face-to-face.
Mount Tiantai alone points to the remote ocean beyond,
spreading its fame everywhere.

平野水寬闊　丹丘連四明　仙都最高秀　群峰聳翠屏
遠遠望何極　矹矹勢相迎　獨標海隅外　處處播嘉名

119

Far up in the distant sky,
there's a cliff-side road high behind clouds.
A waterfall flows down a thousand yards
like a white silk ribbon.
Below is Qixin Cave.
Peacefully at its side is Dingming Bridge.
Imposing its magnificence on the world,
the name of Mount Tiantai is beyond compare.

迥聳霄漢外　雲裏路岧嶢　瀑布千丈流　如鋪練一條
下有棲心窟　橫安定命橋　雄雄鎮世界　天臺名獨超

*120

The Hill of Immortals rises as high as the clouds,
while five other peaks appear low in the distance.
The height of the pagoda surpasses a row of green cliffs,
and an ancient meditation hall enters a rainbow.
As pine needles shake in the wind, Mount Chicheng is magnificent.
When mist spits inside the cave, I get lost on the sorcerer's path,
the blue sky descends, and thousands of mountains and cliffs appear.
Wisteria vines tie the valleys together.

丹丘迴聳與雲齊　空裏五峰遙望低　雁塔高排出青嶂　禪林古殿入虹蜺
風搖松葉赤城秀　霧吐中巖仙路迷　碧落千山萬仞現　藤蘿相接次連谿

121

When I think of this still place,
it is subtle and deep beyond description.
Without wind, vines stir by themselves,
without mist, the bamboo grove is tall and dark.
The valley stream—for whom does it weep?
Mountain clouds come together all of a sudden.
At midday I sit inside my hut—
only then do I realize the sun has risen.

以我棲遲處　幽深難可論　無風蘿自動　不霧竹長昏
澗水緣誰咽　山雲忽自屯　午時庵內坐　始覺日頭暾

122

"Cold Mountain is so strange."
All climbers are afraid.
The moon shines on crystal waters,
winds blow, shuffling the grass.
Withered plum trees blossom with snow,
bare branches fill with leaves of clouds.
Just a touch of rain wakens the spirit—
it doesn't matter if the weather's not clear.

寒山多幽奇　登者皆恆懾　月照水澄澄　風吹草獵獵
凋梅雪作花　杌木云充葉　觸雨轉鮮靈　非晴不可涉

*123

Even if you row a three-winged boat,
or gallop on a thousand-*li* horse,
you cannot reach my home.
I live deep in the countryside,
a rocky gorge far in the mountains
where thunderclouds amass all day.
Other than Lord Confucius,
there's no one here to lend me a hand.

快捲三翼舟　善乘千里馬　莫能造我家　謂言最幽野
巖岫深嶂中　雲雷竟日下　自非孔丘公　無能相救者

124

Far, far, the road to Cold Mountain.
Falling, scattering, the chilled mountain stream.
Quietly, sadly, the birds keep whispering.
Lonely, lonely, nobody here.
Roaring, roaring, wind lashes my face.
Bit by bit, snow covers me up.
Morning after morning, the sun isn't seen.
Year after year, I don't know the spring.

杳杳寒山道　落落冷澗濱　啾啾常有鳥　寂寂更無人
磧磧風吹面　紛紛雪積身　朝朝不見日　歲歲不知春

125

Sitting alone, I often feel anxious.
How long will this yearning last?
Clouds move slowly across the mountain's waistline,
at the mouth of the valley, winds blow chilly and wild.
Monkeys arrive in the swaying trees,
birds fly into the forest and wail.
At this time, melancholy presses against the hair on my temples—
the year draws to an end for this sad old man.

獨坐常忽忽　情懷何悠悠　山腰雲縵縵　谷口風颼颼
猿來樹裊裊　鳥入林啾啾　時催鬢颯颯　歲盡老惆惆

*126

Six sufferings always hang around your neck—
exploring the nine ways to govern is in vain.
Whatever talent I had was lost in a swamp,
having no skills, I close my wormwood door.
The sun is up, though the cliff is dark,
the mist is gone, the valley still in shadow.
This child from a wealthy family possesses nothing,
not even a loincloth.

六極常嬰困　九維徒自論　有才遺草澤　無藝閉蓬門
日上巖猶暗　煙消穀尚昏　其中長者子　個個總無褌

127

Ah, I am poor and sick.
From the start, I've been cut off from family and friends.
There's been no rice in the jar for so long,
only dust fills up my steamer.
My grass-roofed hut cannot help leaking,
the wet bedding is bad for my body.
Don't wonder why I'm this worn down—
a lot of worry can destroy anyone.

吁嗟貧復病　為人絕友親　甕裏長無飯　甑中屢生塵
蓬庵不免雨　漏榻劣容身　莫怪今憔悴　多愁定損人

128

Today I sat in front of a cliff,
until the foggy clouds disappeared.
The single road through the valley was cool.
On the thousand-yard blue peak,
the shadow of morning clouds was still.
A bright moon shines through the night.
On my body there is no dust or filth—
in my heart, why would there be any worry?

今日巖前坐　坐久煙雲收　一道清溪冷　千尋碧嶂頭
白雲朝影靜　明月夜光浮　身上無塵垢　心中那更憂

*129

In vain, I preached the Three Histories
and indulged myself reading the Five Scriptures.
Until I was old, I examined the landowners' records,
though I have always lived as an ordinary person.
Divination pointed to double unhappiness,
a life under the stars of danger and loss.
This is not as good as a tree beside the river
that turns green once a year.

徒勞說三史　浪自看五經　泊老檢黃籍　依前住白丁
筮遭連蹇卦　生主虛危星　不及河邊樹　年年一度青

*130

White clouds stack steep and high,
in the gorge, green waters flow gently.
From this spot, I can hear fishermen,
sometimes drumming on the oars and singing songs.
The sound of their voices is too painful to hear,
it just fills me with sorrow.
Who says a sparrow has no horn?
It can gouge a hole in a house.

白雲高嵯峨　渌水蕩潭波　此處聞漁父　時時鼓棹歌
聲聲不可聽　令我愁思多　誰謂雀無角　其如穿屋何

131

A mountain dweller with a wilting heart
often sighs as the years move on.
He looks hard for a miraculous mushroom,
but even if he finds it, how can he become an immortal?
His grounds are spacious, the clouds start to swirl,
over the forest the bright moon is round.
Why doesn't he leave?
The fragrant cassia keeps him where he is.

山客心悄悄　常嗟歲序遷　辛勤採芝朮　搜斥詎成仙
庭廓雲初卷　林明月正圓　不歸何所為　桂樹相留連

132

The sound of birds chirping is too sad to bear—
I lie down in my grass-thatched hut.
Crimson cherries sparkle and shine,
willow branches hang so softly.
Morning sun embraces the blue peaks,
clouds clear off, washing in the lake's green water.
Who would think I could leave the dusty world,
just charging up Cold Mountain from the south?

鳥語情不堪　其時臥草庵　櫻桃紅爍爍　楊柳正毿毿
旭日銜青嶂　晴雲洗淥潭　誰知出塵俗　馭上寒山南

*133

Why is the mountain so chilly?
It's been this way since ancient times, not just this year.
Snow always remains on the peaks of the range,
the dark forest spewing up mist.
Weeds flourish after midsummer,
leaves fall before autumn begins.
It is here that a man has lost his way—
he looks and looks but cannot see the sky.

山中何太冷　自古非今年　杳嶂恆凝雪　幽林每吐煙
草生芒種後　葉落立秋前　此有沈迷客　窺窺不見天

134

The setting sun glows behind western mountains,
grass and trees are luminous,
but there are dark, misty areas
where pine trees link up with creeping vines.
Within those places are many crouching tigers
who might spot me and charge.
Not having even an inch-long blade in my hand,
how should I not be afraid?

夕陽赫西山　草木光曄曄　復有朦朧處　松蘿相連接
此中多伏虎　見我奮迅鬣　手中無寸刃　爭不懼懾懾

135

I heard sadness cannot be driven away.
I didn't think it was true,
so yesterday morning I pushed it back.
Today it returned, and tangled me up.
Months end, but sadness doesn't.
Years are renewed, and so is sadness.
Who would guess that under my wisteria hat
there is a sadness this old?

聞道愁難遣　斯言謂不真　昨朝曾趁卻　今日又纏身
月盡愁難盡　年新愁更新　誰知席帽下　元是昔愁人

136

Cold Mountain is cold,
ice locks up the stones.
The mountain's green is hidden,
only white snow appears.
The sun rises and shines,
briefly melting the snow.
From now on, the warmth
will nurture this old guest.

寒山寒　冰鎖石　藏山青　現雪白　日出照　一時釋　從茲暖　養老客

137

After a sorrowful year,
spring arrives in the bright color of things.
Mountain flowers smile at green rivers,
blue mist dances in front of cliffs and caves,
while bees and butterflies sing their joy.
I feel so close to the fish and birds,
their company brings no end of happiness—
I cannot sleep past the dawn.

歲去換愁年　春來物色鮮　山花笑淥水　巖岫舞青煙
蜂蝶自云樂　禽魚更可憐　朋游情未已　徹曉不能眠

Alone, I lie down below the cliffs—
even in daytime, steaming clouds don't drift away.
Although my chamber is gloomy beneath a hazy sun,
my mind has cut off its clamor.
In a dream, I play inside the immortals' golden gate,
before my spirit returns across a bridge of stone.
I have hurled away all past quarrels
that banged like a noisy gourd against a tree.

獨臥重巖下　蒸雲晝不消　室中雖曀曀　心裏絕喧囂
夢去游金闕　魂歸度石橋　拋除鬧我者　歷歷樹間瓢

139

Someone dwells on a mountainside
where clouds swirl and mist wraps around.
He wants to make a gift of fragrant herbs,
but the road is far off and difficult to pass.
A heart could grow sad and doubtful
that old age will come with nothing achieved.
People crow and laugh at such a stubborn man,
but he stands alone, faithful and pure.

有人兮山楹　雲卷兮霞纓　秉芳兮欲寄　路漫兮難征
心惆悵兮狐疑　年老已無成　眾喔咿斯蹇　獨立兮忠貞

*140

Cold Mountain is deep,
it fits my heart.
The stones are pure white,
not gold.
Water from the spring resounds
as I strum Bo's lute.
If Ziqi hears it,
he'll recognize the tune.

寒山深　稱我心　純白石　勿黃金　泉聲響　撫伯琴　有子期　辨此音

141

Only white clouds on Cold Mountain,
so still beyond the dusty world.
My mountain home has a grass seat,
the solitary lamp is the moon's bright disk.
My stone bed overlooks the jade pond,
tiger and deer are often my neighbors.
I covet the joy of my secluded dwelling,
where I can always be a person beyond form.

寒山唯白雲　寂寂絕埃塵　草座山家有　孤燈明月輪
石床臨碧沼　虎鹿每為鄰　自羨幽居樂　長為象外人

*142

A hand moves a brush freely,
the body as remarkable as rare jade.
But life comes to an end
and death makes one a nameless spirit.
From ancient times it has been like this,
so here's what you can do:
Come inside the white cloud,
I will teach you the purple mushroom song.

手筆太縱橫　身材極瑰瑋　生為有限身　死作無名鬼
自古如此多　君今爭奈何　可來白雲裏　教爾紫芝歌

*143

Taking my time, I climb to the top of Huading Peak.
A bright sun illuminates the middle of the day.
When I look around in the clear sky,
white clouds fly together with cranes.

閑游華頂上　日朗晝光輝　四顧晴空裏　白雲同鶴飛

144

Since arriving at Tiantai,
so many winters and springs have flown past.
Mountains and waters don't change, but I have grown old—
most of the people I see are from the next generation.

自從到此天台境　經今早度幾冬春　山水不移人自老　見却多少後世人

145

Amidst these cliffs,
there's enough clear wind.
No need to flap the fan,
the cool air passes through.
A bright moon shines,
the white cloud remains.
I sit here alone,
one old man.

重巖中　足清風　扇不搖　涼冷通　明月照　白雲籠　獨自坐　一老翁

PART TWO

EARLY ADDITIONS

Circa Seventh to Eighth Century

*146

You who read my poems,
protect the purity of your heart—
be more modest with your grasping and greed.
Then, what is crooked will straighten out,
driving away unwholesome deeds.
Just take refuge in your true nature
and you'll attain a buddha body today
like a fast-running demon!

凡讀我詩者　心中須護淨　慳貪繼日廉　諂曲登時正
驅遣除惡業　歸依受眞性　今日得佛身　急急如律令

*147

This tree was growing before the forest was born.
If you guess its age, it's twice as old.
Its roots met the changes of hills and ravines,
its leaves were altered by wind and frost.
Everyone laughs at its outer decay,
failing to appreciate the colorful patterns within.
Its bark may have peeled away,
but there is only truth inside.

有樹先林生　計年逾一倍　根遭陵谷變　葉被風霜改
咸笑外凋零　不憐內文彩　皮膚脫落盡　唯有貞實在

*148

I prefer to live in obscurity,
my home beyond the noise and dust of the world.
Treading on weeds, I have made three paths,
seeing clouds as my neighbors in the four directions.
The birds help me to sing,
but when I ask about the dharma, no one replies.
Among these trees of the *saha* world,
how many years make up just one spring!

吾家好隱淪　居處絕囂塵　踐草成三徑　瞻雲作四鄰
助歌聲有鳥　問法語無人　今日娑婆樹　幾年為一春

*149

I usually live in a quiet secluded place,
but there are times I go to Guoqing Monastery
to drop in on Fenggan,
or pay a visit to Shide.
Then, I return alone to my wintry cave,
where there is no one to talk to.
When I look for a limitless source of water,
the source may be limited, but the water is not.

慣居幽隱處　乍向國清中　時訪豐干道　仍來看拾公
獨回上寒巖　無人話合同　尋究無源水　源窮水不窮

150

Longing for pleasure in the mountains,
I wander about without depending on anything.
Day after day I take care of what remains of my body,
quietly not thinking of things to be done.
Sometimes I unroll an ancient buddha's writings.
Often I climb atop stone pavilions
to peer down the thousand-foot cliff below.
Above me a trail of clouds is moored,
the moon is cold, chilly winds howl.
My body is like a lone flying crane.

自羨山間樂　逍遙無倚托　逐日養殘軀　閑思無所作　時披古佛書
往往登石閣　下窺千尺崖　上有雲盤泊　寒月冷颼颼　身似孤飛鶴

*151

My original home is on Tiantai.
The way is cloudy, the mist deep, cutting off visitors.
A thousand-*ren* mountain range is the right place to retreat,
my stone lookout above countless layers of valleys and streams.
Wearing a birch-bark hat and wooden sandals, I stroll beside rivers.
In a leather-and-cloth robe, holding a bramble stick,
　　I circle the mountain.
I realize this floating life is a constantly changing illusion,
but joyous rambling is just so good!

餘家本住在天臺　雲路煙深絕客來　千仞巖巒深可遁　萬重谿澗石樓臺
樺巾木屐沿流步　布裘藜杖繞山回　自覺浮生幻化事　逍遙快樂實善哉

*152

I sit quietly at the edge of the precipice,
the full moon illuminating the heavens.
In its light, countless images appear,
but the disk itself does not actually shine.
Clearly, the spirit is pure,
embodying the subtle and mysterious void.
Because the finger points, I see the moon—
the moon is the essence of mind.

嚴前獨靜坐　圓月當天耀　萬象影現中　一輪本無照
廓然神自清　含虛洞玄妙　因指見其月　月是心樞要

*153

Being greatly foolish in the past
will not make you enlightened today.
Today's poverty
comes from your former life.
If you don't practice in this one,
your future life will be just the same.
If you have no boat between shores,
the vast water is impossible to cross.

生前大愚癡　不為今日悟　今日如許貧　總是前生作
今生又不修　來生還如故　兩岸各無船　渺渺難濟渡

*154

I've sat steadily on Cold Mountain,
absorbed just here for thirty years.
Yesterday, I went to visit close companions,
though most are already in the underground spring.
Gradually, their lives burned out like candles,
they drifted off like water in a stream.
This morning I faced my solitary shadow—
before I knew it, two threads of tears came streaming down.

一向寒山坐　淹留三十年　昨來訪親友　太半入黃泉
漸減如殘燭　長流似逝川　今朝對孤影　不覺淚雙懸

*155

We should admire this good strong man
whose figure inspires real awe.
Not even thirty springs and autumns have passed,
yet he's talented in a hundred different arts.
Wearing a golden breast plate, he competes with other warriors,
then gathers friends together for a feast.
There is only one thing lacking—
he does not transmit the inexhaustible lamp.

可憐好丈夫　身體極棱棱　春秋未三十　才藝百般能
金羈逐俠客　玉饌集良朋　唯有一般惡　不傳無盡燈

*156

If you encounter a demon,
first of all, don't be startled.
Be firm, don't let it in.
If you call out its name, it will go away.
Offer incense to ask for the Buddha's help,
bow deeply to request the sangha's support.
A mosquito biting an iron ox
cannot penetrate with its sting.

若人逢鬼魅　第一莫驚懜　捺硬莫採渠　呼名自當去
燒香請佛力　禮拜求僧助　蚊子叮鐵牛　無渠下觜處

*157

Sailing in a boat of rotten wood
you search for *nimba* fruit.
You journey across the great ocean,
where high surging waves never stop.
With only enough food for one night,
you travel three thousand miles from shore.
Where does such delusion come from?
How sad so much suffering comes to pass.

乘茲朽木船　採彼紅婆子　行至大海中　波濤復不止
唯齋一宿糧　去岸三千里　煩惱從何生　愁哉緣苦起

*158

You leave home to travel countless miles,
carrying a sword to attack the northern barbarians.
If you're victorious, they die.
If you're not, you fall.
Though their lives may not matter to you,
why risk your life?
Let me tell you how to win one hundred battles:
Don't be greedy, that's the best plan.

去家一萬里　提劍擊匈奴　得利渠即死　失利汝即殂
渠命既不惜　汝命亦何辜　教汝百勝術　不貪為上謨

*159

You who greedily seek pleasure don't realize
the calamity of your one hundred years.
What you see is just a mirage or bubbles in water,
soon you will know the body's impermanence and decay.
If your aspiration is as strong as iron,
your heart of the way is genuine.
Just practice intimately, like frost gathering beneath bamboo—
then you'll know how not to bend your spirit.

貪愛有人求快活　不知禍在百年身　但看陽焰浮漚水　便覺無常敗壞人
丈夫志氣直如鐵　無曲心中道自真　行密節高霜下竹　方知不枉用心神

EARLY ADDITIONS · 95

*160

Boars eat dead human flesh,
humans eat the guts of a boar.
The boars don't mind a dead human's odor,
and humans say that boar meat is delicious.
But if we cast dead boars into water,
and dig holes to bury human beings,
they can't eat each other.
A lotus could bloom in boiling water.

豬吃死人肉　人吃死豬腸　豬不嫌人臭　人反道豬香
豬死抛水內　人死掘土藏　彼此莫相啖　蓮花生沸湯

*161

Why do you weep so hard,
your tears dropping like pearls?
Have you just separated,
or lost someone you love?
You suffer so much because you haven't realized
the principle of cause and effect.
You look at the dead body in the cemetery,
but the six paths may not trouble you.

啼哭緣何事　淚如珠子顆　應當有別離　復是遭喪禍
所為在貧窮　未能了因果　塚間瞻死尸　六道不干我

*162

Not practicing the genuine path,
she follows a mistaken one, but calls herself an old woman of the way.
With her shameful mouth, she has little to say to gods and buddhas,
her mind overflowing with jealousy.
Behind people's backs, she eats fish and meat,
while chanting Buddha's name before them.
If she carries on like this,
she can't avoid the river of hell.

不行真正道　隨邪號行婆　口慚神佛少　心懷嫉妒多
背後瞳魚肉　人前念佛陀　如此修身處　難應避奈河

*163

A group of fools,
completely mindless like donkeys,
understand what others say,
but are as greedy and randy as young boars.
It's hard to hazard a guess about them,
since truth turns false when they speak.
Who can even talk with them?
It's better just to stay away.

世有一等愚　茫茫恰似驢　還解人言語　貪淫狀若豬
險巇難可測　實語卻成虛　誰能共伊語　令教莫此居

*164

A man whose family name is Arrogance
was first called Greed, and later on, Dishonest.
He understands nothing,
and whatever he does is despised.
He hates the bitter taste of death,
and only loves the sweetness of living.
Yet he won't stop eating fish,
and never gets tired of meat.

有漢姓傲慢　名貪字不廉　一身無所解　百事被他嫌
死惡黃連苦　生憐白蜜甜　吃魚猶未止　食肉更無厭

*165

Anger is fire in the mind,
it can burn down the forest of merit.
If you want to practice the bodhisattva way,
protect the true mind with patience.

瞋是心中火　能燒功德林　欲行菩薩道　忍辱護真心

*166

You bury your head deeply in idiocy,
and rush into the demon cave of ignorance.
Again and again, I urge you to practice right away,
but you're stubborn, with a dreamy, stupid mind.
Rejecting what Cold Mountain says,
your karma keeps doubling like rushing water.
When your head finally splits in two,
you'll know you're the slave of a thief.

汝為埋頭癡兀兀　愛向無明羅刹窟　再三勸你早修行　是你頑癡心恍惚
不肯信受寒山語　轉轉倍加業汨汨　直待斬首作兩段　方知自身奴賊物

*167

The unwholesome realms are vast,
completely dark without sunlight.
Even if you live for eight hundred years,
you won't experience even half a night.
When I think of all the ignorant people,
my heart hurts deeply.
I urge you to set yourself apart
and recognize the king of dharma.

惡趣甚茫茫　冥冥無日光　人間八百歲　未抵半宵長
此等諸癡子　論情甚可傷　勸君求出離　認取法中王

*168

Heaven is high without limit.
Earth is deep with no end.
Animals live there,
relying on the power of the natural world.
They fight to stuff their bellies, and for warmth,
devouring each other if they can.
Cause and effect are beyond our understanding—
we're like blind children asking the color of milk.

天高高不窮　地厚厚無極　動物在其中　憑茲造化力
爭頭覓飽暖　作計相啗食　因果都未詳　盲兒問乳色

*169

Humming, a man buys fish and meat
to carry home and feed his family.
Why do you kill others
so that you can live?
This isn't the way to paradise,
but will clearly lead you to the depths of hell.
It's just like a commoner who speaks to a broken pestle—
from the beginning it makes no sense.

唄唄買魚肉　擔歸喂妻子　何須殺他命　將來活汝己
此非天堂緣　純是地獄滓　徐六語破堆　始知沒道理

*170

If you buy meat, the blood keeps dripping.
If you buy fish, it keeps flipping.
You wear yourself out, piling up unwholesome deeds,
while your wife and children are so happy and alive.
As soon as you die, she will marry again.
Who would dare to stop it?
One morning, like a broken bed,
the two of you will just come apart.

買肉血瀝瀝　買魚跳鱍鱍　君身招罪累　妻子成快活
纔死渠便嫁　他人誰敢遏　一朝如破床　兩個當頭脫

*171

Someone grabbed hold of a plain sandalwood tree
and called it white sandalwood.
Students of the way are as many as grains of sand,
yet how many of them attain nirvana?
They put down gold to pick up weeds,
though blinding others blinds the self.
Like mounding sand in one place
to make a ball, it's a mess.

有人把椿樹　喚作白栴檀　學道多沙數　幾個得泥洹
棄金卻擔草　謾他亦自謾　似聚砂一處　成團也大難

172

Monks who don't keep the precepts,
Daoists who don't take the medicine of immortality—
since ancient times some wise people
have been buried at the foot of green mountains.

沙門不持戒　道士不服藥　自古多少賢　盡在青山腳

*173

If you want an analogy for birth and death,
compare them with ice and water.
Water freezes and turns into ice,
ice melts and returns to water.
Death never fails to become birth,
being born, you return to death as well.
Ice and water don't cause each other harm.
Together, birth and death are beautiful.

欲識生死譬　且將冰水比　水結即成冰　冰消返成水
已死必應生　出生還復死　冰水不相傷　生死還雙美

*174

There's a bright person in the world
who struggles to speak profoundly.
His three talents are unique,
his six arts surpass all others.
His spirit is outstanding,
and his appearance goes beyond the crowd's.
But without knowing the essence within,
he chases outer objects and remains confused.

世有聰明士　勤苦探幽文　三端自孤立　六藝越諸君
神氣卓然異　精彩超衆群　不識個中意　逐境亂紛紛

*175

The plan changes without limit,
birth and death never cease.
At the river of hell, you're a sparrow,
at the Five Mountains of the Immortals, a dragon fish.
In this muddy world, you become a barbarian's sheep,
in a purer age, the legendary steed Luer.
During a previous era, you were a child of wealth,
but this time, you are simply poor.

變化計無窮　生死竟不止　三途鳥雀身　五岳龍魚已
世濁作羖羺　時清為騄耳　前回是富兒　今度成貧士

*176

Ah, this confused, muddy world,
demons and wise ones live together.
If you say they're of equal kind,
how can we tell them apart?
A fox could pretend to have a lion's power,
be reckless and deceitful while talked about with praise.
But if you temper lead in a furnace,
you'll know for certain it's not gold.

呼嗟濁濫處　羅刹共賢人　謂是等流類　焉知道不親
狐假師子勢　詐妄卻稱珍　鉛礦入爐冶　方知金不眞

*177

What kind of scholar is this
who occasionally drops in at the Southern Court?
Thirty or so years old,
with four or five national exams behind him,
there's not a coin in his bag,
just some yellow scrolls in his carrying box.
When he arrives at a shop where people eat,
he doesn't turn his face away for a second.

個是何措大　時來省南院　年可三十餘　曾經四五選
囊裏無青蚨　篋中有黃絹　行到食店前　不敢暫回面

*178

Layers of cloudy mountains lead to heaven's blue.
The path is remote, the forest deep, no visitors come around.
Viewed from afar, the toad-in-the-moon glows brightly,
close by, birds chirp and sing.
An old man sits on a green cliff
in a small room, letting his hair grow white.
He can't help lamenting both past and present days,
his heartbreak flows like water to the east.

雲山疊疊連天碧　路僻林深無客游　遠望孤蟾明皎皎　近聞群鳥語啾啾
老夫獨坐棲青嶂　少室閑居任白頭　可嘆往年與今日　無心還似水東流

*179

My house is not an ornate building,
the pine forest is my home.
Life passes in an instant,
don't say the myriad things are far away.
If you don't make a raft to cross over,
you'll drift and sink just plucking flowers.
If you don't plant wholesome roots now,
when will you ever see them sprout?

畫棟非吾宅　松林是我家　一生俄爾過　萬事莫言賒
濟渡不造筏　漂淪為採花　善根今未種　何日見生芽

180

The world includes a steady stream of people
who are dull, like wooden-headed dolls.
With no understanding, they say,
"I don't worry about anything."
When asked about the way, they don't know it.
When asked about the Buddha, they don't seek the Buddha.
If pushed for any details, they are dumbfounded.
They're only concerned with their own little place.

世有一等流　悠悠似木頭　出語無知解　云我百不憂
問道道不會　問佛佛不求　子細推尋著　茫然一場愁

181

Whose child is this,
so hated by people?
His mind is stupid and always in a rage,
his drunken eyes covered by his hair.
When he sees the Buddha, he doesn't bow.
When he meets a monk, he doesn't offer a coin.
All he knows is how to slice up a flank of meat.
Other than that, he's completely useless.

個是誰家子　為人大被憎　癡心常憤憤　肉眼醉瞢瞢
見佛不禮佛　逢僧不施僧　唯知打大臠　除此百無能

*182

People think the body is our foundation
with the mind in charge.
If your mind is at its source, it won't be crooked,
if your mind is crooked, the source of life is lost.
There's no escaping this disaster.
How can you say you're too lazy to reflect in the mirror?
If you don't keep the *Diamond Sutra* in mind,
you make bodhisattvas sick.

人以身為本　本以心為柄　本在心莫邪　心邪喪本命
未能免此殃　何言懶照鏡　不念金剛經　卻令菩薩病

*183

There are people with a stingy nature,
but I'm not one of them.
Though a single-layer robe is all I wear for dancing,
I finish up my wine as I sing.
I just try to have a bellyful
without my legs turning numb.
When mugwort grows out of their skulls,
they will certainly feel regret.

自有慳惜人　我非慳惜輩　衣單為舞穿　酒盡緣歌唪
當取一腹飽　莫令兩腳儸　蓬蒿鑽髑髏　此日君應悔

Human life lasts a hundred years,
the Buddha's teaching has twelve parts.
Compassion is like a wild deer,
anger is like a dog in the house.
No matter how hard you chase it, the dog won't go away,
while the deer runs with grace.
If you want to subdue your monkey mind,
listen to the lion's roar.

人生一百年　佛說十二部　慈悲如野鹿　瞋忿似家狗
家狗趁不去　野鹿常好走　欲伏獼猴心　須聽獅子吼

On Cold Mountain, there's a naked insect
with a white body and black head.
Its hands hold two scrolls,
the scriptures of Dao and De.
With neither a pot nor stove,
and going about without wearing clothes,
it always carries the sword of wisdom
to cut down that robber: delusion.

寒山有裸蟲　身白而頭黑　手把兩卷書　一道將一德
住不安金灶　行不齋衣祓　常持智慧劍　擬破煩惱賊

*186

A man who fears his white hair,
and won't abandon his red braided cord,
picks herbs, and tries to become an immortal in vain.
At random, he digs up sprouts from the roots,
but it has no effect for years,
and foolishly he becomes angry and depressed.
It's like a hunter who wears a monk's robe—
from the beginning, it's just not his.

有人畏白首　不肯捨朱紱　採藥空求仙　根苗亂挑掘
數年無效驗　癡意瞋怫鬱　獵師披裰裟　元非汝使物

*187

I see worldly people
scurrying all over the dusty road,
not knowing what's essential.
Why do they rush to the ferry?
Their prosperity lasts just a matter of days,
while time with their loved ones goes quickly.
Even if they have a thousand pounds of gold,
it would be better to be poor in the forest.

我見世間人　茫茫走路塵　不知此中事　將何為去津
榮華能幾日　眷屬片時親　縱有千斤金　不如林下貧

*188

When I think back on places I came across in the past,
as I wandered in search of beautiful spots,
I enjoyed climbing immeasurably high mountains,
and loved drifting in a thousand boats.
I sent off my guest to Lute Valley,
and brought my lute to Parrot Island.
How could I know I would end up beneath a pine tree,
grasping my knees against a howling wind?

憶昔遇逢處　人間逐勝游　樂山登萬仞　愛水泛千舟
送客琵琶谷　攜琴鸚鵡洲　焉知松樹下　抱膝冷颼颼

*189

Don't laugh at this country bumpkin
whose head and cheeks are gawky.
My kerchief is not high enough,
my belt is too long and tight.
It's not that I avoid keeping up with fashion,
but I haven't come up with enough money.
Someday, when I have it,
I'll build a stupa on top of a mountain.

笑我田舍兒　頭頰底繁澀　巾子未曾高　腰帶長時急
非是不及時　無錢趁不及　一日有錢財　浮圖頂上立

*190

One thousand births and ten thousand deaths—when will they stop?
Transmigration confuses the heart.
Not knowing the priceless treasure in the mind,
we travel along like blind donkeys trusting their legs.

千生萬死凡幾已　生死來去轉迷情　不識心中無價寶　猶似盲驢信腳行

*191

What is the saddest thing in the world?
Everything is a raft to cross the Three Rapid River.
Don't you know someone's in a cave beneath the white cloud
whose thin cloth robe is his life?
Even when autumn arrives and leaves fall in the forest,
or when spring comes and trees open their blossoms,
I lie down to sleep without a care in the three realms.
The bright moon and pure wind are my home.

世間何事最堪嗟　盡是三途造罪楂　不學白雲巖下客　一條寒衲是生涯
秋到任他林葉落　春來從你樹開花　三界橫眠閑無事　明月清風是我家

*192

"Since birth, I haven't come and gone,
   until death, I owe neither kindness nor duty."
Words that branch out this far
   harbor danger and bias.
If you accept them even a little,
   it will lead to great deceit.
It's like speaking of building a ladder to the clouds—
   pared down, it makes prickly thorns.

從生不往來　至死無仁義　言既有枝葉　心懷便險詖
若其開小道　緣此生大偽　詐說造雲梯　削之成棘刺

*193

One jar is made of cast metal,
   another from kneading clay.
It's up to you to see them,
   so you know which is solid and true.
If you know there are two types of jars,
   you should know there's not just one kind of karma.
Examine what brought about your birth,
   and realize your practice today.

一瓶鑄金成　一瓶埏泥出　二瓶任君看　那個瓶牢實
欲知瓶有二　須知業非一　將此驗生因　修行在今日

*194

How pitiable, the disease of sentient beings!
You never grow tired of savoring your feast.
Steaming pork rubbed with garlic and soy paste,
roasting duck sprinkled with pepper and salt,
removing the bones from raw fish,
while grilling the skin on meat—
you ignore the suffering of other beings
to enjoy the sweetness of your life.

憐底眾生病　餐嘗略不厭　蒸豚揾蒜醬　炙鴨點椒鹽
去骨鮮魚膾　兼皮熟肉臉　不知他命苦　只取自家甜

195

How can you avoid death by reading?
How can you escape poverty by reading?
What's the good of knowing letters?
Does it make you better than other people?
Those who don't know letters
have nowhere to take shelter.
When you soak pungent herbs in garlic and soy paste,
if you leave out the amounts, it can taste bitter and hot.

讀書豈免死　讀書豈免貧　何以好識字　識字勝他人
丈夫不識字　無處可安身　黃連揾蒜醬　忘計是苦辛

*196

I see someone who deceives others,
just like pouring water in a basket and running away.
In a single breath he heads for home,
but what is left in the basket?
I see someone else who's deceived by others.
He's like a leek in the garden,
day after day cut by a knife,
yet its original nature remains.

我見瞞人漢　如籃盛水走　一氣將歸家　籃裏何曾有
我見被人瞞　一似園中韭　日日被刀傷　天生還自有

*197

Above Cold Mountain's peak, the moon's lone disk
illuminates the clear sky; nothing else appears.
Honor this priceless natural treasure,
hidden in the five *skandhas* of your drowning body.

寒山頂上月輪孤　照見晴空一物無　可貴天然無價寶　埋在五陰溺身軀

*198

My original home is Cold Mountain,
where I dwell in a stone cave, free from trouble.
When I perish, the ten thousand phenomena will leave no trace.
When I stretch out, I flow everywhere into one billion worlds.
Light rises, illuminating the mind ground,
not a single thing appears before me.
I know the wish-granting jewel—
once you learn how to use it, everywhere is whole.

我家本住在寒山　石巖棲息離煩緣　泯時萬象無痕跡　舒處周流遍大千
光影騰輝照心地　無有一法當現前　方知摩尼一顆珠　解用無方處處圓

*199

What do worldly people grieve?
Pain and pleasure entwine without end,
birth and death come and go for many eons.
East, west, south, and north—whose house is it?
Zhang, Wang, Li, and Zhao are temporary names.
The six paths and the river of hell are as crooked as flax—
because the hosts within fail to cut them off,
in the end, they run astray and invite transmigration.

世人何事可吁嗟　苦樂交前勿底涯　生死往來多少劫　東西南北是誰家
張王李趙權時姓　六道三途事似麻　只為主人不了絕　遂招遷謝逐迷邪

Don't you see, the dew that drips in the morning
disappears by itself in the shining sun?
Human life is like this.
The Southern Continent is where we live,
don't let this chance pass you by.
Right now, let the three poisons disperse.
Enlightenment is not separate from delusion—
let everything disappear, leaving nothing behind.

不見朝垂露　日爍自消除　人身亦如此　閻浮是寄居
切莫因循過　且令三毒袪　菩提即煩惱　盡令無有餘

You're high spirited
with a brave appearance.
You can shoot through seven layers of armor,
and read five columns of characters at a glance.
In the past, you slept on a tiger-head pillow.
Long ago, you sat on an ivory couch.
But if you don't have that one thing,
you are as frozen as frost.

精神殊爽爽　形貌極堂堂　能射穿七札　讀書覽五行
經眠虎頭枕　昔坐象牙床　若無阿堵物　不啻冷如霜

*202

I live in a village
with no father or mother,
no given name, family name, or number.
People call me Zhou or Wang,
and no one teaches me.
Being poor and lowly is ordinary,
but I love having my true mind,
solid as a diamond.

我住在村鄉　　無爺亦無娘　　無名無姓第　　人喚作張王
並無人教我　　貧賤也尋常　　自憐心的實　　堅固等金剛

203

The water is crystal clear,
the bottom visible just as it is.
When there's not a thing in your mind,
things won't turn you around.
If your mind doesn't arouse delusion,
this will never change.
When you understand this,
you'll know there is no other side.

水清澄澄瑩　　徹底自然見　　心中無一事　　萬境不能轉
心既不妄起　　永劫無改變　　若能如是知　　是知無背面

204

Talking about food never fills you up,
discussing clothing won't keep away the cold.
To be full, you must eat food,
wearing clothes, you will avoid the cold.
If you don't investigate thoroughly,
seeking the Buddha is impossible.
Returning to your original mind is itself Buddha—
don't try other than this.

說食終不飽　說衣不免寒　飽吃須是飯　著衣方免寒
不解審思量　只道求佛難　回心即是佛　莫向外頭看

*205

Aimlessly, I close the mugwort door and sit.
Time flies quickly like sparks off flint.
I have only heard that people turn into ghosts,
but have never seen cranes become immortals.
Thinking of this, what can I say?
Follow your karma and pity yourself.
When I look outside the city walls,
ancient cemeteries are plowed into rice fields.

徒閉蓬門坐　頻經石火遷　唯聞人作鬼　不見鶴成仙
念此那堪說　隨緣須自憐　回瞻郊郭外　古墓犁為田

Sentient beings are hard to speak about.
Why are they so confused?
Their two heads are evil birds.
In their minds are three poisonous snakes.
These create obstacles,
and cause lots of trouble.
Just lift up your hand and snap your fingers:
Homage to the Buddha!

衆生不可說　何意許顛邪　面上兩惡鳥　心中三毒蛇
是渠作障礙　使你事煩拏　舉手高彈指　南無佛陀耶

*207

I enjoy an ordinary way of living
amongst mist, vines, and rocky caves,
where the feeling of the wild moves freely through the vastness.
For a long time, I've accompanied the white cloud.
There is a path, but it does not go through to worldly realms.
With no mind, what is there to climb?
I spend the night sitting alone on the stone floor,
while the full moon rises over Cold Mountain.

自樂平生道　煙蘿石洞間　野情多放曠　長伴白雲間
有路不通世　無心孰可攀　石床孤夜坐　圓月上寒山

With so many rare treasures aboard,
they journey on a large broken boat.
The bow has lost its mast,
the stern is without a tiller.
Spinning whichever way the wind blows,
high and low, they follow the breaking waves.
How can they reach the shore
without trying hard to sit upright?

如許多寶貝　海中乘壞舸　前頭失卻桅　後頭又無柁
宛轉任風吹　高低隨浪簸　如何得到岸　努力莫端坐

*209

People in the three realms are sluggish,
those in the six paths are lost.
Greedy for things and following carnal desires,
their wicked minds are like jackals and wolves—
they fly to hell swift as an arrow.
How can they bear such terrible suffering?
They pass from morning to night
without discerning what is wise and virtuous,
or knowing good from bad.
They're just like pigs and sheep.
They talk to each other like wood to stone,
get crazed with jealousy and envy,
but don't see their own faults.
They're like boars crouching in a cage.
Without realizing they're repaying their debts,
they just laugh at the ox that keeps turning the mill.

三界人蠢蠢　六道人茫茫　貪財愛淫欲　心惡若豺狼
地獄如箭射　極苦若為當　兀兀過朝夕　都不別賢良
好惡總不識　猶如豬及羊　共語如木石　嫉妒似顛狂
不自見己過　如豬在圈臥　不知自償債　卻笑牛牽磨

*210

Humans live in blinding dust,
like insects in a bowl.
All day we go around and around
and never get out of the bowl.
But, it's impossible to become an immortal,
and delusion is endless.
Time flows by like water—
in an instant we are old.

人生在塵蒙　恰似盆中蟲　終日行繞繞　不離其盆中
神仙不可得　煩惱計無窮　歲月如流水　須臾作老翁

*211

I have six brothers.
Among them, one was bad.
I couldn't beat him,
and when I yelled at him, he didn't care.
In every respect, what difference did it make?
He indulged in material wealth, easy sex, and slaughtering.
When he saw something he liked, he had to have it—
his greed was greater than a demon's.
Our father hated seeing him,
our mother disliked him and felt no joy.
Yesterday I grabbed him
and let loose my feelings without holding back.
I took him to where there was no one else
and spoke to him face-to-face.

"You should change your ways.
If the wagon overturns, get it back on track.
If you don't believe and accept what I say,
we'll hate and kill each other.
If you accept my warning,
together we'll look for a way to live."
Since then, we live in harmony.
He even surpasses a bodhisattva.
He's learned to temper iron in the furnace,
and has refined the iron of all three mountains.
Until this very day, his life is peaceful and serene—
everyone admires him.

我有六兄弟　就中一個惡　打伊又不得　罵伊又不著
處處無奈何　耽財好淫殺　見好埋頭愛　貪心過羅剎
阿爺惡見伊　阿娘嫌不悅　昨被我捉得　惡罵恣情掣
趁向無人處　一一向伊說　汝今須改行　覆車須改轍
若也不信受　共汝惡合殺　汝受我調伏　我共汝覓活
從此盡和同　如今過菩薩　學業攻爐冶　煉盡三山鐵
至今靜恬恬　眾人皆贊說

*212

Wearing rags comes from earlier karma,
don't blame your current life.
If you say it's caused by the shape of your tomb,
you are extremely foolish
and will end up a ghost.
How could you make your family poor?
This is easily understood.
Why are you so unaware?

襤縷關前業　莫訶今日身　若言由塚墓　個是極癡人
到頭君作鬼　豈令男女貧　皎然易解事　作麼無精神

*213

Let me say to those who eat meat,
when eating, nothing can tempt you to stop.
This life is what you sowed in your last one,
your future life is what you cultivate today.
If you merely take today's delicacy
without fearing grief in your next life,
you are like an old rat who gets into a rice jar—
though he's eaten his fill, his head can't get out.

寄語食肉漢　食時無逗遛　今生過去種　未來今日修
只取今日美　不畏來生憂　老鼠入飯甕　雖飽難出頭

*214

I see the Yellow River—
how many times has it been clear?
It flows fast as an arrow,
the human world just a floating weed.
Stupidity is rooted in karma,
the pit of ignorance and delusion.
Transmigration over eons
is created by getting lost in blindness.

我見黃河水　凡經幾度清　水流如急箭　人世若浮萍
癡屬根本業　無明煩惱坑　輪回幾許劫　只為造迷盲

*215

I urge you young children
to quickly flee the burning house.
Three carts are outside the gate
to give you a ride so you don't wander about.
A crossroads awaits on the ground,
though in the heavens all things are empty.
The ten directions have no up or down,
coming and going depends on east and west.
If you understand the meaning of this,
you're free wherever you are.

余勸諸稚子　急離火宅中　三車在門外　載你免飄蓬　露地四衢坐
當天萬事空　十方無上下　來去任西東　若得個中意　縱橫處處通

*216

Worldly affairs continue on and on,
but people won't stop their greed.
It's like grinding away a great stone—
when will it come to an end?
The four seasons keep changing,
the eight calendar points rush by like a stream.
Let me tell you, master of a house on fire:
Ride the white ox into an open field.

世事繞悠悠　貪生未肯休　研盡大地石　何時得歇頭
四時周變易　八節急如流　為報火宅主　露地騎白牛

*217

Where Cold Mountain lives in retreat
is cut off from strangers passing through.
At times, I meet birds in the forest
and together we sing mountain songs.
Sacred grasses spread across valleys,
old pines pillow against high rugged stone.
You may see a person of ease there,
resting in the mountain shade.

寒山棲隱處　絕得雜人過　時逢林內鳥　相共唱山歌
瑞草聯谿谷　老松枕嵯峨　可觀無事客　憩歇在巖阿

*218

If you have no clothes, go look for them,
don't scheme with a fox to get its fur.
If you have no food, go out and pick some,
don't conspire with a sheep so you can have a feast.
If you take their hide and meat,
their hearts will hurt and grieve.
Such actions make you lose your decency,
you will always be short of food and clothing.

無衣自訪覓　莫共狐謀裘　無食自採取　莫共羊謀羞
借皮兼借肉　懷嘆復懷愁　皆緣義失所　衣食常不周

*219

Sitting just here on a flat stone,
the valley stream is bitter cold.
Quietly, I appreciate its utter beauty,
my empty cave lost in the mist.
At this place, where I rest in joy,
the slanting sun makes long shadows of the trees.
When I observe my mind ground
a lotus comes out of the muddy water.

盤陀石上坐　谿澗冷淒淒　靜玩偏嘉麗　虛巖蒙霧迷
怡然憩歇處　日斜樹影低　我自觀心地　蓮花出淤泥

220

Naturally, I long for a way-seeking companion,
companions of the way often become very close.
At times, I meet someone who penetrates the source.
Whenever I speak with a Zen practitioner,
we discuss profound matters on a moonlit night,
searching for reality until daybreak.
By letting go of all traces,
you'll surely know the original person.

本志慕道倫　道倫常獲親　時逢杜源客　每接話禪賓
談玄月明夜　探理日臨晨　萬機俱泯跡　方識本來人

*221

Let me suggest you stop running around.
Don't upset Old Man Yama.
If you fail, you will cross the Three Rapid River,
where your bones will be crushed by a thousand beatings.
For a long time, you'll be a prisoner in hell,
far from this life's path.
Strive hard, and trust what I say—
take hold of the treasure inside your own robes.

勸你休去來　莫惱他閻老　失腳入三途　粉骨遭千搗
長為地獄人　永隔今生道　勉你信餘言　識取衣中寶

*222

Far above the tallest peak,
when I look around, there is no boundary.
I sit alone, though no one understands.
A solitary moon shines on Cold Spring,
but the moon is not in it.
The moon is just free in the blue sky.
Even if I sing just one tune,
what I sing is not Zen.

高高峰頂上　四顧極無邊　獨坐無人知　孤月照寒泉
泉中且無月　月自在青天　吟此一曲歌　歌終不是禪

*223

A deer lives deep in the forest,
drinking water, eating grass,
and stretching its legs while it sleeps beneath a tree.
How lovely to have no worries.
If it was kept tied up in a luxurious room,
offered delicious and abundant meals,
it would not take a bite all day.
Soon it would look withered and frail.

鹿生深林中　飲水而食草　伸腳樹下眠　可憐無煩惱
系之在華堂　肴膳極肥好　終日不肯嘗　形容轉枯槁

*224

Even if you store up rhinoceros horns,
wear a tiger's eyeball,
drive away evil with a peach branch,
or make a garlic necklace;
even if you warm your belly with dogwood wine
or drink wolfberry soup to empty your mind,
in the end you cannot avoid death,
but have sought eternal life in vain.

縱你居犀角　饒君帶虎睛　桃枝將闢穢　蒜殼取為瓔
暖腹茱萸酒　空心枸杞羹　終歸不免死　浪自覓長生

*225

Cold Mountain cave doesn't leak,
its rock is solid and secure.
When the eight winds blow, it doesn't budge.
The ancients have passed down its wonders.
So serene, it's good for peaceful dwelling,
free from people's sneers and blame.
The solitary moon glows through the night,
the sun disk always returns to shine.
Tiger Hill merges with Tiger Valley,
there's no need to send for each other.
In the world there are king's assistants,
don't take them for Lord Zhou or Shao.
Since I escaped to Cold Rock
I've been happy, singing and laughing a long, long time.

寒山無漏巖　其巖甚濟要　八風吹不動　萬古人傳妙　寂寂好安居
空空離譏誚　孤月夜長明　圓日常來照　虎丘兼虎谿　不用相呼召
世間有王傅　莫把同周邵　我自遁寒巖　快活長歌笑

*226

Someone laughed at my poems,
but my poems match the classical standards.
I'm not bothered by Zhou's commentary,
and how can I use Mao's interpretation?
I don't regret that it's the rare person who understands.
If I let my poems follow *do* and *re*
I'd have endless problems.
If they happen to be met by clear-eyed people,
they'll certainly spread through the world.

有人笑我詩　我詩合典雅　不煩鄭氏箋　豈用毛公解　不恨會人稀
只為知音寡　若遣趁宮商　餘病莫能罷　忽遇明眼人　即自流天下

*227

There are people in the world with vast knowledge
who are foolish and suffer bitterly in vain.
Not seeking a wholesome future
they only know how to cause harm.
Their five betrayals and ten unwholesome actions
make them intimate with the three poisons.
Once they die and enter hell
what they know is as useless as silver kept in the storehouse.

世有多解人　愚癡徒苦辛　不求當來善　唯知造惡因
五逆十惡輩　三毒以爲親　一死入地獄　長如鎖庫銀

*228

Long ago, someone traveled the great ocean,
determined to get a wish-granting jewel.
As soon as he reached the inner chamber of the dragon palace,
he cut through the golden barrier chain,
which alarmed the dragon king, though he was safe inside.
The warrior swung his sword and searched to the stars,
    but he couldn't find the jewel.
Having done what he could, he returned and entered the gate,
where he realized the bright jewel was his original mind.

昔年曾到大海遊　爲采摩尼誓懇求　直到龍宮深密處　金關鎖斷主神愁
龍王守護安耳裏　劍客星揮無處搜　賣客却歸門內去　明珠元在我心頭

229

Leisurely, I went to visit an esteemed monk,
amid layers and layers of misty mountains.
The master intimately pointed to the path of my return.
The moon hangs like a disk-shaped lamp.

閑自訪高僧　煙山萬萬層　師親指歸路　月掛一輪燈

230

If you have a poem by Cold Mountain in your house,
it's better than reading a scroll of sutras.
Write it on a folding screen
and take a look from time to time.

家有寒山詩　勝汝看經卷　書放屏風上　時時看一遍

PART THREE

LATER ADDITIONS

Circa Late Eighth to Ninth Century

231

I see Tiantai peak,
solitary above the entire range.
Pines sway in the wind, bamboo stalks rustle,
the moon appears, tides flow out and in.
Scanning the green slopes below,
I discuss the profound principle with the white cloud.
Though the feeling of the wild is in mountains and waters,
truly, I long for a companion of the way.

目見天臺頂　　孤高出衆群　　風搖松竹韻　　月現海潮頻
下望青山際　　談玄有白雲　　野情便山水　　本志慕道倫

*232

In the month when farmers rest, avoiding the heat,
who's around to enjoy some wine?
The rows of wild fruit in disarray,
a few of us surround the barrel.
With a reed mat for my seat,
and a banana leaf as a plate,
after drinking, I sit with my jaw on my arm.
Mount Sumeru seems as small as a pellet.

田家避暑月　　斗酒共誰歡　　雜雜排山果　　疏疏圍酒樽
蘆莒將代席　　蕉葉且充盤　　醉後支頤坐　　須彌小彈丸

233

Since leaving home,
I finally understand how to nurture life.
Fully stretching and bending my limbs,
trying to listen to my six senses,
wearing a coarse robe from spring into winter,
eating brown rice, morning and evening—
today I practice thoroughly,
hoping to encounter the Buddha.

自從出家後　漸得養生趣　伸縮四肢全　勤聽六根具
褐衣隨春冬　糲食供朝暮　今日懇懇修　願與佛相遇

*234

I've always heard that Shakyamuni Buddha
received Dipankara Buddha's prediction of enlightenment.
Dipankara and Shakyamuni are explained
as wisdom before and wisdom after,
though the essence of before and after is not different.
Within the difference, there is no difference.
One buddha is all buddhas—
mind is the ground of tathagata.

常聞釋迦佛　先受然燈記　然燈與釋迦　只論前後智
前後體非殊　異中無有異　一佛一切佛　心是如來地

235

I notice that people who are sharp and wise observe,
then understand the meaning.
Without depending on texts,
they directly enter the ground of tathagata.
Because they don't chase after entangled forms,
their minds don't give rise to delusion.
When this does not appear,
inside or outside, there is nothing extra.

我見利智人　觀者便知意　不假尋文字　直入如來地
心不逐諸緣　意根不妄起　心意不生時　內外無餘事

236

An emerald stream—pure spring water,
Cold Mountain's moonlight is luminous.
In silence I realize my spirit is clear.
Seeing the empty sky, things grow even more still.

碧澗泉水清　寒山月華白　默知神自明　觀空境逾寂

237

Facing the valley, where I look at my reflection in the stream,
or the cliff, where I sit on a large flat stone,
my mind is like a solitary cloud, completely free.
Vast and unhindered, why would I search for worldly things?

我向前溪照碧流　或向巖邊坐盤石　心似孤雲無所依　悠悠世事何須覓

*238

In Sengyao's paintings, I see his eccentric personality—
among those born in the Liang Dynasty, he was so ingenious.
Daozi was exceptionally spontaneous.
Both of them painted well, with strong brush movement,
and though each was masterful, their true spirits differed.
High-spirited Sengyao made dragons fly and demons run,
but even if he could paint the empty sky and the common world,
there's no way he could paint Master Zhi.

餘見僧繇性希奇　巧妙間生梁朝時　道子飄然為殊特　二公善繪手毫揮
逞畫圖真意氣異　龍行鬼走神巍巍　饒邈虛空寫塵跡　無因畫得志公師

*239

How balmy it was yesterday!
This place is so lovely.
Up above, there's a path through peach and apricot trees,
down below, a sandbank of orchids and irises.
Also, there's a woman here who dresses in fine silk.
Inside the house, she wore a green-feathered hair ornament.
We wanted to speak to each other,
but for the longest time, we couldn't find the words.

昨日何悠悠　場中可憐許　上為桃李徑　下作蘭蓀渚
復有綺羅人　舍中翠毛羽　相逢欲相喚　脈脈不能語

*240

Layers of mountains and rivers are exquisite,
misty clouds enclose the subtle green.
The storm brushes away a moist silk hat,
while dew soaks my straw raincoat.
My feet tread in shoes made for wandering
with an old wisteria branch in my hand.
I see beyond the dusty world—
what's the point of dreaming?

層層山水秀　煙霞鎖翠微　嵐拂紗巾濕　露沾蓑草衣
足躡游方履　手執古藤枝　更觀塵世外　夢境復何為

*241

Since I first came to live on Cold Mountain,
so many years have passed.
Trusting fate, I escaped to forests and natural springs
where I live at ease and see things freely.
No one comes to visit Cold Cliff,
the white cloud is so often obscured.
With a bed made of thin grass
and the blue sky for my cover,
I rest my head happily on a stone pillow
and follow the changes of heaven and earth.

粵自居寒山　曾經幾萬載　任運遁林泉　棲遲觀自在
寒巖人不到　白雲常靉靆　細草作臥褥　青天為被蓋
快活枕石頭　天地任變改

242

My abode is in a cave
that doesn't contain a single thing.
Clean, empty, and grand,
it shines brightly every day.
I eat vegetables to nurture my thin body,
and wrap a leather-and-cloth garment around this illusory self.
Even if one thousand sages should appear,
I am with the original buddha.

餘家有一窟　窟中無一物　淨潔空堂堂　光華明日日
蔬食養微軀　布裘遮幻質　任你千聖現　我有天真佛

243

In the midst of a thousand clouds and countless waters
there is an idle person.
By day, he roams the green mountains,
at night, he returns to sleep beneath the cliff.
Quickly, the seasons pass
in serenity, with no worldly bonds.
How joyful! What does he depend upon?
Quiet, like a large autumn river.

千雲萬水間　中有一閑士　白日游青山　夜歸巖下睡
倏爾過春秋　寂然無塵累　快哉何所依　靜若秋江水

244

At times, people seek the cloud path,
but it's obscure and leaves no trace.
The mountains are high and steep,
broad streams hold little light.
Green peaks overlap front to back,
white clouds gather from the west and east.
If you want to know where the cloud path is,
it's in the open sky.

時人尋雲路　雲路杳無蹤　山高多險峻　澗闊少玲瓏
碧嶂前兼後　白雲西復東　欲知雲路處　雲路在虛空

Revere this legendary mountain—
how can the seven treasures compare?
Beneath the moon, chilly winds blow through the pines
as wisps of clouds arise.
So many mountain ridges layer into each other
for miles and miles around!
The valley stream is quiet and clear—
I'm not done with this boundless joy.

可貴一名山　七寶何能比　松月颼颼冷　雲霞片片起
唘匝幾重山　迴還多少里　谿澗靜澄澄　快活無窮已

246

Since I escaped to Cold Mountain,
I eat wild fruit to stay alive.
In this ordinary life, why should I worry?
I follow the conditions of the fleeting world.
Days and months flow by like a river,
time passes like sparks off flint.
Even if heaven and earth were to move,
I'm at ease, sitting inside my cave.

一自遁寒山　養命餐山果　平生何所憂　此世隨緣過
日月如逝川　光陰石中火　任你天地移　我暢巖中坐

247

I live on a mountain,
others don't know.
Inside the white cloud
it's always peaceful and serene.

我居山　勿人識　白雲中　常寂寂

*248

Hanyuan is deep and fine.
No one comes this way.
The white cloud is high, the cave quiet,
on a green cliff a lone monkey howls.
Where could I feel more at one?
Free from worry, I age naturally.
My appearance changes with the advancing seasons,
but my heart jewel remains.

寒巖深更好　無人行此道　白雲高岫閑　青嶂孤猿嘯
我更何所親　暢志自宜老　形容寒暑遷　心珠甚可保

When I was young, I was too lazy to read.
By thirty, achieving anything was still to come.
After my hair turned white, I got my first official job,
though I was no more than an assistant to ten high officers.
I don't know the many types of millet
I pay for the house where I lie down.
I drink some wine, chant a poem, and go to sleep.
I expect I'll be like this till I'm one hundred.

少年懶讀書　三十業由來　白首始得官　不過十卿尉
不知多種黍　供此伏家費　打酒詠詩眠　百年期髣髴

250

My whole life I've been too lazy to do anything.
I hate weighty things, and prefer what is light.
Other people study business,
but I have only one volume of a sutra.
I don't intend to mount it on a scroll,
and avoid those who come to hold it up.
If someone is sick, I talk with them about medicine.
With skillful means, I help sentient beings.
My mind has no hindrance—
where is it not awake?

一生慵懶作　憎重只便輕　他家學事業　餘持一卷經　無心裝褾軸
來去省人擎　應病則說藥　方便度眾生　但自心無事　何處不惺惺

*251

I see home leavers
who have not entered the study of leaving home.
If you want to truly leave home,
your mind should be pure with no binding rope.
Clear, beyond wondrous mysteries,
thusness itself does not depend on anything.
It allows freedom in the three realms
and doesn't abide in the four types of birth.
A person beyond doing, free of obstruction,
wanders with true joy.

我見出家人　不入出家學　欲知真出家　心淨無繩索　澄澄絕玄妙
如如無倚托　三界任縱橫　四生不可泊　無為無事人　逍遙實快樂

252

The place I used to walk,
I see again after seventy years.
Those I used to know do not come and go,
but remain buried in their tombs.
Now, with my hair turned white,
I still keep watch over clouds and mountains.
Let me say to those in the future:
Why not study the words of the ancients?

昔日經行處　今復七十年　故人無來往　埋在古塚間
餘今頭已白　猶守片雲山　為報後來子　何不讀古言

253

Hermits flee from the human world,
many of them heading for the mountains to sleep.
Green vines are sparse in the foothills,
where a blue brook murmurs
leisurely at ease.
Pure and relaxed, I spend my time
free from the stain of worldly things,
my mind serene as a white lotus.

隱士遁人間　多向山中眠　青蘿疏麓麓　碧澗響聯聯
騰騰且安樂　悠悠自清閑　免有染世事　心靜如白蓮

254

Cherish this Cold Mountain,
where the white cloud is always at ease.
Monkeys cry out playfully in the way,
but tigers howl, entering the human realm.
I walk alone, stepping on stones,
singing to myself and grasping wisteria vines.
The pine wind is pure, *hyooo hyooo.*
Birds twitter, *cheep cheep.*

可重是寒山　白雲常自閑　猿啼暢道內　虎嘯出人間
獨步石可履　孤吟藤好攀　松風清颯颯　鳥語聲喧喧

*255

I live quietly under Cold Rock,
often wondering about its magic.
I take my basket to collect mountain greens,
and bring it back with picked fruit.
To eat vegetables, I sit down on a reed mat
and peck away at purple mushrooms.
Rinsing my gourd bowl in a clean puddle,
I boil things together into a thin soup.
Then I wrap up in a leather coat, sit in the sun,
and slowly read an ancient's poems.

棲遲寒巖下　偏訝最幽奇　攜籃採山茹　挈籠摘果歸　蔬齋敷茅坐
啜啄食紫芝　清沼濯瓢缽　雜和煮稠稀　當陽擁裘坐　閑讀古人詩

256

Yesterday, I climbed to the top of a peak
and looked down a thousand-foot cliff.
I approached a tree trunk standing at its edge,
rattled by the wind, with two branches torn apart.
Hurled about by rain until it decayed,
exposure to the sun had dried it into dust.
Ah, see how this once-flourishing tree
is now just a pile of ash.

昨日游峰頂　下窺千尺崖　臨危一株樹　風擺兩枝開
雨漂即零落　日曬作塵埃　嗟見此茂秀　今為一聚灰

257

What a shame this hundred-year-old house
leans left and right.
Broken and scattered
trees lie about in disarray,
bricks and tiles have fallen to the ground.
Its decay is hard to bear seeing.
A raging wind blows over the ruins—
it can't be rebuilt at all.

可惜百年屋　左倒右復傾　墻壁分散盡　木植亂差橫
磚瓦片片落　朽爛不堪停　狂風吹驀塌　再豎卒難成

258

I see that people in the world
are born, and then they die.
Those who were sixteen just yesterday morning,
with vigorous spirits and hearts,
are now past seventy,
with waning strength and a haggard look.
We're just like flowers on a spring day
that open in the morning and in the evening decline.

我見世間人　生而還復死　昨朝猶二八　壯氣胸襟士
如今七十過　力困形憔悴　恰似春日花　朝開夜落爾

*259

How pitiful—people in the floating life!
How many days do they feel lighthearted?
Morning after morning they have no leisure time.
Year after year they don't reflect on getting old.
For the sake of getting food and clothing,
they let their minds grow deluded.
In chaos, year after year,
they come and go on the three unwholesome paths.

可嘆浮生人　悠悠何日了　朝朝無閑時　年年不覺老
總為求衣食　令心生煩惱　擾擾百千年　去來三惡道

260

I see worldly people,
each competing with vigor.
One day they will suddenly die
and acquire just one plot of land,
four feet wide
and twelve feet long.
If you know how to come out
and compete with spirit,
I'll erect a tombstone
and inscribe your name.

我見世間人　個個爭意氣　一朝忽然死　只得一片地　闊四尺
長丈二　汝若會出　來爭意氣　我與汝　立碑記

*261

Since ancient times, wise people
have not been known for their long lives.
They are born, and then they die,
all of them turning to ashes and dust.
Their bones pile up like Mount Vipula,
while those who are left shed an ocean of tears.
Only their empty names remain.
How can they avoid the cycle of birth and death?

自古諸哲人　不見有長存　生而還復死　盡變作灰塵
積骨如毗富　別淚成海津　唯有空名在　豈免生死輪

*262

I heard there was a jade tree
on Mount Tiantai.
For a long time, I wanted to climb to it,
but didn't know the stone bridge path.
This made me despair—
pretty soon the sun will set on my humble abode.
Today, as I look in the mirror,
my white hair hangs sadly down.

我聞天臺山　山中有琪樹　永言欲攀之　莫繞石橋路
緣此生悲嘆　幸居將已暮　今日觀鏡中　颯颯鬢垂素

263

Why am I sad for so long?
Human life is like a morning mushroom.
How can this last for decades?
Both new and old wither and fall—
of course I feel sad.
It's a sorrow so hard to bear,
how will I ever endure it?
I'll take my body back to hide in the mountains.

何以長惆悵　人生似朝菌　那堪數十年　新舊凋落盡
以此思自哀　哀情不可忍　奈何當奈何　托體歸山隱

*264

Yesterday I visited Yunxiaguan Temple
where some venerable Daoist hermits suddenly appeared,
casually wearing star-shaped hats and moon-ornamented coats.
They all said they live among mountains and waters.
I asked about the magic arts of the immortals,
and they explained that if a comparison was made,
these would be unsurpassable.
"Wondrous medicine is always mysterious.
It protects against death while waiting for the white crane to arrive.
All Daoists depart on the back of a fish."
Afterward, I thought about it,
and decided it made no sense.
Just watch an arrow fly through the air—
in a moment it falls to the ground.
Even if you become a sorcerer,
it's like a spirit trying to stay with its corpse.
When the essence of the mind moon is clear,
how could the myriad things compare?
If you want to know the sorcerer's medicine for immortality,
the original spirit inside the body is it!
Don't study with those who wear yellow scarves,
clinging to your stupidity.

昨到雲霞觀	忽見仙尊士	星冠月帔橫	盡云居山水	餘問神仙術
云道若為比	謂言靈無上	妙藥必神秘	守死待鶴來	皆道乘魚去
餘乃返窮之	推尋勿道理	但看箭射空	須臾還墜地	饒你得仙人
恰似守尸鬼	心月自精明	萬象何能比	欲知仙丹術	身內元神是
莫學黃巾公	握愚自守擬			

*265

In a broken-down grass hut,
filled with fire and thick smoke,
I said to a group of young children,
"Were you just born?
Look! There are three carts outside."
I wanted to get them out, but they kept filling their stomachs
and wouldn't budge.
They were all so foolish and stubborn.

摧殘荒草廬　其中煙火蔚　借問群小兒　生來凡幾日
門外有三車　迎之不肯出　飽食腹膨脝　個是癡頑物

*266

There are ordinary people in the world
who are neither bad nor good.
They don't know they are hosts,
but wander as guests from place to place.
Because they merely pass the time,
they are stupid slivers of meat.
Though they have a sacred platform,
they're just like hired hands.

世有一般人　不惡又不善　不識主人公　隨客處處轉
因循過時光　渾是癡肉臠　雖有一靈臺　如同客作漢

I hear in the kingdom of Liang
there were four types of wise teachers—
Masters Baozhi and Wanhui,
four sorcerers, and Layman Fu.
They all aspired to spread the Buddha's teaching.
As messengers of the Tathagatha,
they constructed temple buildings
and were devoted to the Buddha's principle.
Although this was so,
problems started to mount up—
getting far from the way,
they tried to fix east when west was broken.
This didn't work,
much damage came about, and little benefit.
There were noisy proclamations, but nothing took shape.
Having arrived at this place, where could they go?

自聞梁朝日　四依諸賢士　寶志萬廻師　四仙傅大士
顯揚一代教　作持如來使　造建僧伽藍　信心歸佛理
雖乃得如斯　有為多患累　與道殊懸遠　折西補東爾
不達無為功　損多益少矣　有聲而無形　至今何處去

268

Since ancient times, sages
encouraged trusting the self,
but human beings are not equal—
high and low, sharp and dull,
they don't accept the authentic Buddha.
They push for power in vain and only make trouble,
not knowing the pure, unstained mind
is the seal of the dharma king.

自古多少聖　叮嚀教自信　人根性不等　高下有利鈍
真佛不肯認　置功枉受困　不知清淨心　便是法王印

269

Let me say to those who practice the way:
Seeking worthless things exhausts your mind.
People have a spiritual essence,
beyond words or description.
When you call on it, it responds clearly,
when it is hidden, you don't know where it is.
Keep it well,
don't let it be stained.

報汝修道者　進求虛勞神　人有精靈物　無字復無文
呼時歷歷應　隱處不居存　叮嚀善保護　勿令有點痕

I went down the mountain for a while
to go into the town beyond the city moat.
I happened to see a group of women
who looked elegant and beautiful,
wearing brocade hair ornaments,
lipstick, and face powder.
Their golden bracelets were inlaid with silver flowers,
their fine silk robes were purple and crimson.
Their bright faces were like the immortals,
fragrance rose from their sashes.
People who passed by looked back,
foolish attraction infecting their hearts.
Saying they are beautiful beyond compare,
they were transported by their fantasies,
like dogs biting on dry bones,
vainly licking their own lips and teeth.
In the same way, not reflecting and understanding
is no different from being animals.
Now these women have become white haired,
old and coarse like ghosts,
and those with doglike minds from the beginningless past
cannot leap to liberation.

儂家暫下山　入到城隍里　逢見一群女　端正容貌美　頭戴蜀樣花
燕脂塗粉膩　金釧鏤銀朵　羅衣緋紅紫　朱顏類神仙　香帶氛氳氣
時人皆顧盼　癡愛染心意　謂言世無雙　魂影隨他去　狗咬枯骨頭
虛自舐脣齒　不解返思量　與畜何曾異　今成白髮婆　老陋若精魅
無始由狗心　不超解脫地

His mind high as a mountain peak,
this person does not bow down to others.
He elucidates and lectures on Vedic scripture,
and can discourse on the Three Teachings,
yet, without shame,
he breaks the precepts and violates the guidelines.
He says he's above human law,
and claims he's the best.
Stupid people all praise him,
while wise ones clap their hands and laugh.
In the world of mirages and flowers of emptiness,
who can avoid life and old age?
It's better not to understand so many things,
but to sit quietly, free from worry.

心高如山嶽　人我不伏人　解講圍陀典　能談三教文　心中無慚愧
破戒違律文　自言上人法　稱為第一人　愚者皆贊嘆　智者撫掌笑
陽焰虛空花　豈得免生老　不如百不解　靜坐絕憂惱

272

The great ocean waters are boundless.
Innumerable fish and dragons
eat each other up.
What stupid lumps of flesh!
When we don't free the mind,
delusion keeps rising like smoke.
The moon of self-nature is clear and bright,
illuminating everywhere without end.

大海水無邊　魚龍萬萬千　遞互相食啖　冗冗癡肉團
為心不了絕　妄想起如煙　性月澄澄朗　廓爾照無邊

273

A sturdy person
does not act carelessly,
but powerfully raises up an iron rock mind
and directly takes the path of enlightenment.
Don't follow crooked ways
that only lead to hardship.
Instead of searching for the buddha fruit,
just realize the essence of mind.

男兒大丈夫　作事莫莽鹵　勁挺鐵石心　直取菩提路
邪路不用行　行之枉辛苦　不要求佛果　識取心王主

274

Honor your own nature—
alone, it has no companion.
If you look for it, you can't see it,
it goes in and out without a gate.
If you shrink it, it exists in one square inch.
If you stretch it, it is everywhere.
If you don't trust and treasure it,
you cannot encounter it.

可貴天然物　獨一無伴侶　覓他不可見　出入無門戶
促之在方寸　延之一切處　你若不信愛　相逢不相遇

275

How many people there are at Tiantai
who don't know Cold Mountain.
Not knowing my true meaning,
they say my words make no sense.

多少天臺人　不識寒山子　莫知真意度　喚作閑言語

I've noticed that ordinary, ignorant people
store up lots of grain and riches,
drink wine, and eat other living beings,
saying, "I deserve what's mine."
They don't know the depth of hell,
but seek only the happiness of the heavenly realm.
Their unwholesome karma is as massive as Mount Vipula.
How can they avoid its disastrous poison?
When these owners of such abundance suddenly die,
people compete to grieve beside their pillows,
and monks offer incense while chanting
empty prayers for the spirit's good fortune.
There's not a scrap of merit in it.
They're just a gang of fake baldies,
unlike those who have always known
not to fall into the prison of darkness.
A raging storm cannot move a tree.
When the mind is genuine, there is neither fault nor blessing.
I offer these words to many, many people—
please read this poem again and again.

我見凡愚人	多畜資財穀	飲酒食生命	謂言我富足	莫知地獄深
唯求上天福	罪業如毗富	豈得免災毒	財主忽然死	爭共當頭哭
供僧讀文疏	空是鬼神祿	福田一個無	虛設一群禿	不如早覺悟
莫作黑暗獄	狂風不動樹	心真無罪福	寄語冗冗人	叮嚀再三讀

*277

I encourage those of you in the three realms
not to ignore the way.
If you lack the principle, others will deceive you.
If the principle is strong, how could you be deceived?
The murky world overflows with people
who are just like wood lice.
Can't you see that a person of no preference
alone is free beyond compare?
Immediately, return to the source,
leaving conditions in the three realms to arise.
With purity, enter the stream of thusness—
don't drink from the waters of ignorance.

勸你三界子　莫作勿道理　理短被他欺　理長不奈你
世間濁濫人　恰似鼠粘子　不見無事人　獨脫無能比
早須返本源　三界任緣起　清淨入如流　莫飲無明水

Thinking back over twenty years,
I slowly walk to Guoqing Monastery.
Everyone at Guoqing says,
"Cold Mountain is a fool."
Why suspect that someone's a fool?
They suspect, but don't know how to think.
They don't know themselves,
so how can they understand me?
They don't bow and ask questions,
but even if they did, what's the use?
Someone once shouted at me.
Of course, I knew what he was saying,
though I didn't reply.
That worked really well.

憶得二十年　徐步國清歸　國清寺中人　盡道寒山癡　癡人何用疑
疑不解尋思　我尚自不識　是伊爭得知　低頭不用問　問得復何為
有人來罵我　分明了了知　雖然不應對　卻是得便宜

279

People more or less
devise countless schemes, seeking fame and gain,
greedily trying to make prosperity bloom
as they toil for privilege and wealth.
Their minds never rest,
but swirl like smoke in the air.
Their families are close-knit
and with just a word, everyone agrees.
Yet, in less than seventy years,
they melt like ice or crumble like tiles—
everyone dies and all matters come to rest.
Who can inherit
mud balls soaked in water?
We know it just makes no sense.

多少般數人　百計求名利　心貪覓榮華　經營圖富貴　心未片時歇
奔突如煙氣　家眷實團圓　一呼百諾至　不過七十年　冰消瓦解置
死了萬事休　誰人承後嗣　水浸泥彈丸　方知無意智

Cold Mountain says things repeatedly,
like a confused madman.
When something happens, I face it and speak up.
Many people resent me,
but my mind is true, and my words straightforward.
A true mind has no hidden side.
At the time of death, when you cross the river to hell,
who is this shifty person?
On the dark journey to the Yellow Spring
you are shackled by your karma.

寒山出此語　復似顛狂漢　有事對面說　所以足人怨
心真出語直　直心無背面　臨死度奈河　誰是嘍羅漢
冥冥泉臺路　被業相拘絆

281

If we look at worldly things,
overall, the details are known,
but not every matter is so readily grasped.
Everyone loves to seek the easiest way,
defending it until bad things become preferred,
slandering, even if truth is opposed.
Thus, know that all groundless speech
has something behind it.
Just experience hot or cold yourself,
without trusting other people's lips.

推尋世間事　子細總皆知　凡事莫容易　盡愛討便宜　護即弊成好
毀即是成非　故知雜濫口　背面總由伊　冷暖我自量　不信奴脣皮

282

A visitor criticized Cold Mountain,
"Your poems make no sense!"
I told him, "But, look at the ancients,
humble and unashamed of being poor."
He just laughed and said,
"Your words are far too careless and loose.
I hope you'll get up to date—
money is the most pressing matter."

客難寒山子　君詩無道理　吾觀乎古人　貧賤不為恥
應之笑此言　談何疏闊矣　願君似今日　錢是急事爾

283

Fear the suffering of transmigration
that comes and goes like swirling dust.
Without ceasing, you spin in the six paths
like ants in wild confusion.
Even if your head and the holes in your face change,
you can't get away from your past self.
Understand the darkness of hell right away,
don't let your mind-nature be obscured.

可畏輪回苦　往復似翻塵　蟻巡環未息　六道亂紛紛
改頭換面孔　不離舊時人　速了黑暗獄　無令心性昏

284

A pair of ducks live in their nest,
a male and female couple.
They hold a flower in their beaks and eat it together,
then smooth each other's feathers in turn.
For fun, they fly into a trailing mist,
then return home to the shore by the water's edge.
They love and enjoy the place they were born,
and wouldn't invade the phoenix's pond.

止宿鴛鴦鳥　一雄兼一雌　銜花相共食　刷羽每相隨
戲入煙霄裏　宿歸沙岸湄　自憐生處樂　不奪鳳凰池

285

On Cold Mountain there's a house
with nothing inside that divides it.
The six gates lead left and right,
from the hall you can see the blue sky.
Every room is completely bare,
from the east wall to the west.
With not a thing in it,
there's nothing to withhold from others.
When cold comes, I make a small fire.
When hunger comes, I boil vegetables and eat.
Ignorant, old country people
keep large rice fields and houses.
These just create the karma of hell.
Once you enter it, how can it ever end?
Think it over.
If you do, you'll get the point.

寒山有一宅　宅中無闌隔　六門左右通　堂中見天碧
房房虛索索　東壁打西壁　其中一物無　免被人來惜
寒到燒軟火　饑來煮菜吃　不學田舍翁　廣置田莊宅
盡作地獄業　一入何曾極　好好善思量　思量知軌則

*286

Don't blame others for their faults,
or praise yourself for your merit.
Practice what you should practice,
letting go of what needs letting go.
A high income brings great worry with it.
Speak deeply, and be wary of superficial relations.
If you listen thoughtfully,
even a child can understand.

不須攻人惡　何用伐己善　行之則可行　卷之則可卷
祿厚憂積大　言深慮交淺　聞茲若念茲　小子當自見

*287

Steaming sand to make rice,
being thirsty, and then digging a well,
or strenuously polishing a rough tile—
how could this make it a mirror?
From the start, Buddha's teachings are universal.
The nature of all things is true thusness.
Just contemplate this thoroughly,
without a useless struggle.

蒸砂擬作飯　臨渴始掘井　用力磨碌磚　那堪將作鏡
佛說元平等　總有真如性　但自審思量　不用閑爭競

288

I hear the nation's minister has a high salary.
He wears a red and purple robe,
a hairpin and a braided cord.
Having wealth and nobility in every respect,
he still covets prosperity without shame.
Servants and horses fill his property,
gold and silver pile high in his treasury.
This idiotic good fortune helps for a while,
but it just buries him in hell.
When he suddenly dies, everything stops.
His family weeps by his pillow,
not knowing that disaster is on the way.
The house will stand in ruins as the cold winds howl.
Without a grain of millet to eat,
the pain of freezing and starvation is very harsh.
All of this comes from being so out of touch.

常聞國大臣　朱紫簪纓祿　富貴百千般　貪榮不知辱
奴馬滿宅舍　金銀盈帑屋　癡福暫時扶　埋頭作地獄
忽死萬事休　男女當頭哭　不知有禍殃　前路何疾速
家破冷颼颼　食無一粒粟　凍餓苦淒淒　良由不覺觸

289

The daughter in a house to the east
is about eighteen years old.
Young men from the west come by
to compete for her hand in marriage.
She fries mutton, boils animals,
is shameless with her guests, and takes part in the killing.
Enjoying herself now, she smiles and laughs,
but she'll know hardship and weeping in the end.

我見東家女　年可有十八　西舍競來問　願姻夫妻活
烹羊煮眾命　聚頭作淫殺　含笑樂呵呵　啼哭受殃抉

290

In the countryside there are many mulberry fields,
cows and calves fill the barns.
Do the people believe in cause and effect?
Sooner or later they flay their animals,
then consume the rest.
For now, these people make their living,
but they'll end up in paper pants or patched loincloths,
frozen or starving to death.

田舍多桑園　牛犢滿廄轍　肯信有因果　頑皮早晚裂
眼看消磨盡　當頭各自活　紙褲瓦作褌　到頭凍餓殺

*291

Humans are like black-headed insects
trying to make a thousand-year tune
like cast iron for a threshold.
When demons see this, they clap their hands and laugh.

人是黑頭虫　剛作千年調　鑄鐵作門限　鬼見拍手笑

292

Let me offer you good people some words,
so you may reconsider your thinking.
If you master the way and see true nature,
true nature is itself tathagata.
You already possess the original truth,
but practice and realization keep changing places.
If you give up the root and just chase twigs,
you remain simply hopeless.

寄語諸仁者　復以何為懷　達道見自性　自性即如來
天真元具足　修證轉差回　棄本卻逐末　只守一場呆

*293

Laugh at the cave of five *skandhas*
where four snakes live together.
In the pitch black, there is no illuminating lamp.
The three poisons keep switching back and forth
while a team of six thieves
steal the dharma treasure jewel.
But if you cut off this troop of demons,
your peace and tranquility will revive.

可笑五陰窟　四蛇共同居　黑暗無明燭　三毒遞相驅
伴黨六個賊　劫掠法財珠　斬卻魔軍輩　安泰湛如蘇

*294

Crush the Five Mountains into powder,
Mount Sumeru one inch high.
Turn the great ocean into a drop of water,
inhale it into your mind field.
Plant seeds of a bodhi tree
that shelters heaven within heaven.
I speak to you who long for the way,
don't get trapped by the ten entanglements.

五嶽俱成粉　須彌一寸山　大海一滴水　吸入在心田
生長菩提子　遍蓋天中天　語汝慕道者　慎莫繞十纏

*295

Let me tell you young nobles,
I heard that Shi Qinu
had eight hundred boy servants,
with water wheels set up in thirty places.
Below his house he kept fish and birds.
On the upper floor, various flutes were played.
When his head was placed beneath the killer's blade,
his foolish mind was on Luzhu, the flute player he adored.

傳語諸公子　聽說石齊奴　僮僕八百人　水碓三十區
舍下養魚鳥　樓上吹笙竽　伸頭臨白刃　癡心為綠珠

*296

You should fear the wheel of the three realms
that never rests for a moment.
If you try to poke your head out of it,
you will soon sink and drown.
Even if you reach the realm beyond nonthinking,
it is due to your good deeds in the past.
How can you realize the true source
that you recognize suddenly and forever?

可畏三界輪　念念未曾息　纔始似出頭　又卻遭沈溺
假使非非想　蓋緣多福力　爭似識真源　一得即永得

*297

In my village there is a house,
but the house has no true master.
On the ground, one inch of weeds grows,
watered by single drops of dew.
Fire burns six thieves
while the wind blows in dark clouds and rain.
When we thoroughly look for the original person,
it's a pearl sewn in the back of a robe.

餘鄉有一宅　其宅無正主　地生一寸草　水垂一滴露
火燒六個賊　風吹黑雲雨　子細尋本人　布裹真珠爾

298

Some people in the world like to do many things,
study broadly, and know a lot,
but they don't realize their original nature,
and are far from the way.
If you can clarify what things really are,
what's the use of wishing in vain?
Once you completely understand your own mind,
the Buddha's insight opens.

世有多事人　廣學諸知見　不識本真性　與道轉懸遠
若能明實相　豈用陳虛願　一念了自心　開佛之知見

*299

I see people in the world
who are dignified, with good manners and appearance,
yet they don't return the kindness of their parents.
What is the root of their thinking?
They even fail to return money borrowed from others.
Only after they're born with hooves will they feel sorry.
All people cherish their wives and children,
but these don't take care of their grandparents.

Siblings who are like enemies
are unsatisfied for a long time.
I recall when I was a young boy,
I prayed to the gods that I would grow up.
Now, I have become a unfilial man.
By and large, the world is like this.
We buy meat and eat it alone,
then wipe our mouths and say, "I feel so free!"

People brag openly of being sly,
clever beyond compare,
but when hell's jailer stares at them in anger
they realize for the first time it's too late.
They pick out a buddha, burn fine incense,
choose a monk, take refuge, and make offerings,
though when an arhat begs in front of their gates,
they drive him away as someone they can't use.

Without awakening, you can't be a true person.
No one has ever said you can.
People send letters to invite renowned monks,
offering alms and entreating in several ways.
Yunguang looked like a good dharma teacher,

but he wore horns on his head.
If you don't have everyday mind,
neither sages nor the wise will appear to you.

Ordinary people and sages are all mixed together.
I advise you to stop being led by appearances.
My dharma is wondrous and difficult to understand,
but it is revered by heavenly dragons.

我見世間人　堂堂好儀相　不報父母恩　方寸底模樣
欠負他人錢　蹄穿始惆悵　個個惜妻兒　爺娘不供養
兄弟似冤家　心中長悵怏　憶昔少年時　求神願成長
今為不孝子　世間多此樣　買肉自家噇　抹觜道我暢
自逞說嘍羅　聰明無益當　牛頭努目瞋　始覺時已暴
擇佛燒好香　揀僧歸供養　羅漢門前乞　趁卻閑和尚
不悟無為人　從來無相狀　封疏請名僧　儭錢兩三樣
雲光好法師　安角在頭上　汝無平等心　聖賢俱不降
凡聖皆混然　勸君休取相　我法妙難思　天龍盡回向

300

On a thousand-year-old stone is an ancient's trace.
Before a ten-thousand-foot cliff is one speck of sky.
When the bright moon shines, it always glows purely—
don't bother asking if it's in the west or east.

千年石上古人蹤　萬丈巖前一點空　明月照時常皎潔　不勞尋討問西東

*301

In the past, I struggled and was poor.
Night after night I'd count other people's possessions.
Today, I deeply believe
I should take charge of my affairs.
By digging, I uncovered a hidden treasure—
a pure, fine jewel.
Then came a blue-eyed stranger
who secretly tried to buy it and take it away.
I said to him,
"This jewel is priceless."

昔日極貧苦　夜夜數他寶　今日審思量　自家須營造
掘得一寶藏　純是水精珠　大有碧眼胡　密擬買將去
餘即報渠言　此珠無價數

I'm speaking to those who have left home.
What kind of people are called home leavers?
You seek luxury and stoke your own livelihood.
You inherit schools of those with patched robes,
but enjoy eating delicacies, and sweetening your beaks.
Your crooked minds flatter and hook other people.
All day long you perform rites in the practice hall,
hold sutra books, and conduct services for merit.
You offer incense to the gods and buddhas,
strike the bells and chant loudly together,
but you spend your time learning how to grind up guests,
while day and night you're not even supposed to lie down.
Since you only love money and things,
your minds are not free.
When you see virtuous people,
you hate them and put them down.
It's like comparing donkey shit to fine incense.
You cause the Buddha so much pain!

語你出家輩　何名為出家　奢華求養活　繼綴族姓家　美舌甜唇觜
諂曲心鉤加　終日禮道場　持經置功課　爐燒神佛香　打鐘高聲和
六時學客舂　晝夜不得臥　只為愛錢財　心中不脫灑　見他高道人
卻嫌誹謗罵　驢屎比麝香　苦哉佛陀耶

*303

When I look again at home leavers,
some are upright and others are not.
Those with the highest integrity
have their morality admired by gods.
Even the king shares his carriage seat,
and lords receive them with a bow.
They can be a field of benefaction—
worldly people should treasure them.

Those foolish people far beneath them
are deceptive and always looking for gain.
You can quickly perceive their murky goals.
They have an idiotic love of sex and property,
though they wear the monk's robe.
They rent their lands to get food and clothing,
charging interest for oxen and plows.
They're dishonest no matter what they do.
Morning after morning they commit criminal acts,
while their hips and backs make them suffer.
They're unable to think in wholesome ways,
and suffer the immeasurable pains of hell.
Once they feel a little ill,
they lie in bed for three years.
Although they, too, have buddha nature,
they are ignorant thieves.

Take refuge in Buddha,
seek Maitreya far and wide.

又見出家兒　有力及無力　上上高節者　鬼神欽道德　君王分輦坐
諸侯拜迎逆　堪為世福田　世人須保惜　下下低愚者　詐現多求覓
濁濫即可知　愚癡愛財色　著卻福田衣　種田討衣食　作債稅牛犁
為事不忠直　朝朝行弊惡　往往痛臀脊　不解善思量　地獄苦無極
一朝著病纏　三年臥床席　亦有真佛性　翻作無明賊　南無佛陀耶
遠遠求彌勒

304

I see someone with great knowledge
who uses his mind all day long.
He stands at a fork in the road and shouts out,
deceiving everyone.
This only creates the dregs of hell,
not true practice.
When impermanence suddenly arrives,
he'll know he has squandered his life.

我見多智漢　終日用心神　岐路逞嘍囉　欺慢一切人
唯作地獄滓　不修正直因　忽然無常至　定知亂粉粉

305

There's one group of people in the world
who truly deserve to be laughed at.
They leave home and wear themselves out
deceiving laypeople, yet calling it the way.
Although they wear robes of renunciation,
their robes are infested with fleas.
It would be better if they returned
to mind itself.

世間一等流　誠堪與人笑　出家弊己身　誑俗將為道
雖著離塵衣　衣中多養蚤　不如歸去來　識取心王好

*306

Whenever I see a wheel-turning king,
he is always surrounded by a thousand people.
With ten virtues he teaches in the four directions.
He is graced by many of the seven treasures
that adorn and protect him
with solemnity and goodness.
But, once his good karma wears out,
he'll be like a sick bird living in the rushes,
or an insect on an ox's neck,
receiving the karma of the six paths.
How much more so for ordinary people?
Life is impermanent and can't last long.
Birth and death are like whirling fire,
transmigration as widespread as flax or straw.
If you don't realize this right away,
you'll end up a crooked, hollow old man.

我見轉輪王　千子常圍繞　十善化四天　莊嚴多七寶
七寶鎮隨身　莊嚴甚妙好　一朝福報盡　猶若棲蘆鳥
還作牛領蟲　六趣受業道　況復諸凡夫　無常豈長保
生死如旋火　輪回似麻稻　不解早覺悟　為人枉虛老

*307

I see people turning sutras
who depend on others' words for understanding.
Your mouth turns, but not your mind—
mind and mouth betray each other.
If your mind is true and not crooked
you won't create entanglements.
Just for now, reflect on yourself,
don't look to others instead.
If you become the host within,
you'll know there's no inside or outside.

我見人轉經　依他言語會　口轉心不轉　心口相違背　心真無委曲
不作諸纏蓋　但且自省躬　莫覓他替代　可中作得主　是知無內外

308

Those who are always taken advantage of by others,
stand your ground and spare yourself the misery,
or when you are old you won't have a choice—
others will have pushed you aside.
You'll go to the top of a wild mountain
and want to throw away your life for nothing.
It's like fixing the pen after the sheep are gone—
in the end you'll lose all hope.

為人常吃用　愛意須慳惜　老去不自由　漸被他推斥
送向荒山頭　一生願虛擲　亡羊罷補牢　失意終無極

Aged and sick, I feel more than a hundred years old.
Though my face is yellow, my hair white,
I still love to live in the mountains.
Wrapped in a leather-and-cloth robe,
I go along with the changing conditions.
Why should I envy people with clever looks?
Those who wear out their minds chasing fame and fortune
have a hundred types of greed driving their bodies.
Their illusory lives are like lamps burning out.
Won't their bodies already be buried in tombs?

老病殘年百有餘　面黃頭白好山居　布裘擁質隨緣過　豈羨人間巧樣模
心神用盡為名利　百種貪婪進己軀　浮生幻化如燈爐　塚內埋身是有無

*310

No one makes it up
Cold Mountain road.
If you can get here,
call out ten names.
Cicadas chirp,
but there are no noisy crows.
Yellow leaves fall,
white clouds sweep across the sky.
There are many rock piles,
these mountains are deep.
I live alone,
known as "Good Guide."
Pay attention,
how do I look?

寒山道　無人到　若能行　稱十號　有蟬鳴　無鴉噪　黃葉落
白雲掃　石磊磊　山隩隩　我獨居　名善導　子細看　何相好

311

This white whisk with a sandalwood handle
is fragrant throughout the day.
Soft as swirling mist,
it floats like a drifting cloud.
When offered with a bow, it withstands the heat,
when held high, it removes the dust.
At times, in the abbot's room,
it points the way for someone who has strayed.

白拂栴檀柄　馨香竟日聞　柔和如卷霧　搖拽似行雲
禮奉宜當暑　高提復去塵　時時方丈內　將用指迷人

*312

Dressed in flowers in the sky
and tortoise hair shoes,
I hold a bow made of rabbit horn
to shoot the demon of ignorance.

身著空花衣　足躡龜毛履　手把兔角弓　擬射無明鬼

313

Now, I bow
to the unsurpassable king of dharma,
who offers compassion with great joy,
whose name is chanted in the ten directions.
Sentient beings depend upon
his diamond wisdom body.
Bowing, free from attachment—
our teacher, the great dharma king.

我今稽首禮　無上法中王　慈悲大喜捨　名稱滿十方
眾生作依怙　智慧身金剛　頂禮無所著　我師大法王

314

People nowadays who see Cold Mountain
all say I'm crazy.
They don't look at the face
above this humble robe.
They don't understand what I'm saying,
and I don't speak their language.
All I can say to those who pass by:
"Try to come to Cold Mountain."

時人見寒山　各謂是風顛　貌不起人目　身唯布裘纏
我語他不會　他語我不言　為報往來者　可來向寒山

315

Cold Mountain
is forever this way.
Living alone
beyond birth and death.

寒山子　長如是　獨自居　不生死

Notes

Organized by Poem Numbers

3. *I have made my home*: Meaning "I have decided to live here following the *I Jing*'s (*I-ching*'s) divination.

   White clouds embracing dark stone: This line is taken from a poem by Xie Lingyun (385–433) of the Liu Song Dynasty, included in *Wen Xuan* (Selected Literature), fascicle 26. Iritani and Matsunaga, 10.

   those with cauldrons and chimes: Indicating wealthy people who host feasts with musical presentations.

   there's no merit in your worthless reputation: Reference to one of the nineteen ancient poems included in *Wen Xuan* (Selected Literature), fascicle 29. Iritani and Matsunaga, 10.

4. *Yellow Emperor*: A legendary emperor of ancient China. Regarded as the one who established the calendar, music, letters, and medicine. A book of medicine attributed to him is revered in Daoism.

   Laozi: Also Lao-tzu or Lao Tse. A great thinker of the Zhou Dynasty (403–256 B.C.E.), regarded as the founder of Daoism. The *Daode Jing* (*Tao-te Ching*) is attributed to his authorship.

6. *Abandon your carriage and follow the wisdom of your wife*: A king of Chu during the Spring and Autumn Period (776–403 B.C.E.) asked a wise man, Zizhong of Yuling, to be prime minister, but following advice from his wife, Zhizhong declined the offer and took a humble job.

   A humble cart is pulled by devoted children: The poet Tao Yuanming (365?–427) of the East Jin Dynasty was invited to visit the governor, who offered to send a carriage, but Yuanming chose to ride on a humble cart pulled by his two sons and one of his students.

10. *When she plays her lute beneath the moon*: In *Liezi*, there is a story of a wandering singer named Han'e who was selling her singing on

a street in the kingdom of Qi. Even after she left, the resounding tune of her voice was heard for three days. Hanshan calls it three months.

14. This poem is written in the voice of a female entertainer in a pleasure quarter. Handan was the capital city of the Zhao Kingdom during the Warring Period (403–222 B.C.E.), situated in present-day Henan Province. Known in ancient times as a town of songs and dances with beautiful women.

18. *Luoyang*: The capital city of the Sui Dyanasty, also the eastern capital of the Tang Dynasty. Situated north of the River Luo (present-day Henan Province).

19. *Luoyang*: See above note.

23. *imperial field*: Pinling—known as the burial mound of Emperor Zhao of the Han Dynasty (on the throne 86–80 B.C.E.). It became an imperial hunting ground located northwest of Chang'an.

25. *Dong*: Don Xian, a favorite young boy of Emperor Ai (reigning 6 B.C.E.–1 C.E.) of the Han Dynasty.

30. *Xian*: The capital city of the Qin Empire (221–207 B.C.E.). Also, it means Chang'an. This poem may refer to the destruction of the city at the time of Hanshan.

34. *nine holes*: Eyes, ears, nostrils, mouth, anus, and genital.
This poem is based on a parable in *Zhuangzi* about Chaos meeting the kings of the South Sea and the North Sea, who made a gift of holes drilled in Chaos's body, which caused him to die.

36. *who is modest*: Literally meaning "keeping her gaze low."
Handan: See note on poem 14.

37. *Qi and Chu*: Qi was a kingdom in northeast China (1122–386 B.C.E.) in the Spring and Autumn Period; Chu was a kingdom in south China (704–222 B.C.E.) from the Spring and Autumn Period to the Warring Period.
Qin and Wei: Qin was the first unified empire of China (221–207 B.C.E.); Wei was a kingdom in central northern China (679–631) in the Zhou Period. This story is found in *Liezi*. Iritani and Matsunaga, 152.

38. *Trying to put a square peg in a round hole*: A reference to the "Under the Heaven" part of *Zhuangzi*.

Hualiu: One of the two renowned horses owned by King Mu (on the throne 1001–946 B.C.E.) of the Zhou Dynasty. This line has a direct reference to a line in the "Autumn Water" part of *Zhuangzi*.

39. *White Rabbit*: A sorcerer mentioned in the Daoist classic *Baopuzi*.

40. This poem refers to a story of Yansi, who served as a guard at the time of King Wen (reigning 180–157 B.C.E.) of the Han Dynasty.

42. *Zhuangzi*: Also spelled Chuang-tzu. A renowned Daoist thinker during the Warring Period (770–222 B.C.E.). Author of *Zhuangzi*.

white crane: Symbol of immortality.

If I starve on Mount Souyang as a devoted follower: After the Yin Dynasty was destroyed circa 1100 B.C.E., two courtiers, Boyi and Shuqi, went into exile on Mount Souyang, saying, "We will not eat millet from the Zhou Kingdom." As a result, they starved to death. *Shiji* (The Historical Records), fascicle 61.

44. *nine heavens*: The center and eight directions of the sky.

remain in complete darkness, never to return: Refers to a poem by Cao Zhi (192–232) of the Wei Dynasty, included in *Wen Xuan* (Selected Literature), fascicle 21.

45. *Eastern Mountain of Death*: Mount Tai, one of the five great mountains of China. It is believed that it is where people's spirits go after death.

Northern Cemetery: A cemetery in the suburbs of Luoyang, where many lords and retainers were buried since the Han Dynasty.

49. *five-ideograph poems*: The poetic form with five ideographs per column, and the last ideographs of even-numbered columns rhyming, was the most common poetic form in the Sui and Tang Dynasties. The capacity to compose such poems was essential for passing a national examination for civil officials.

50. *a bitter peach*: A spoiled fruit that will make the crane sick.

51. *the lady of the Lu family*: A girl married to Lu according to the poem, "Water in the River," attributed to Emperor Wu of the kingdom of Liang (464–549).

53. *If you are bound to get an iron bit in your mouth*: If you have acted in unwholesome ways and are destined to be reborn as a horse or a cow.

54. *"Don't keep a swallow nest at your house"*: Meaning that the intimacy of the swallow pair may make you lonelier.

56. *Han*: Han Dynasty, 206 B.C.E.–23 C.E.

61. This poem corresponds to a passage in fascicle 56 of the Daoist scripture *Yunji Qiqian* (Cloud Box Seven Tallies), compiled by Zhang Junfang of the Song Dynasty. Iritani and Matsumura, 116.

64. *Empress Jiapo*: Married to Emperor Hui of the kingdom of Jin (265–420).
    Laozi: See note on poem 4.
    Wei's child: Wei's daughter was beautiful and Emperor Hui (see note above) wanted to marry her, but the marriage never took place.
    Zhong's daughter was extremely ugly: Zhong's daughter, Lichun, was very bad looking, but it is said that when she met King Xuan of the kingdom of Qi (479–501), she discussed the four dangers and was asked to be his queen.

66. *Lord Zhou*: Son of the founding emperor of the Zhou Dynasty (122–294 B.C.E.). He established the protocol and music of the nation.
    Confucius: 552?–479 B.C.E. Educator of the Spring and Autumn Period. *Spring and Autumn* is attributed to him.
    ancient Yang's crane: In the Jin Period (265–420), a man named Yang trained a crane to perform, but the crane was dull and disappointing.

68. *Wutu*: Meaning "Tiger."
    Wanna: Meaning "Chubby."
    flips an earthen spool: In ancient times, when a boy was born, he was given a jade to play with, and when a girl was born, she was given a tile.

71. *Red Sparrow Avenue*: A main street in the capital city of Chang'an of the Tang Dynasty (present-day Shaanxi Province).

72. *yellow bark*: A Chinese cork tree with yellow leaves and bark that are bitter and are used as medicine.

73. *Their wealth has made them rich in stupidity*: This line is from a poem by Zhang Xie of the West Jin Kingdom (265–313), included in *Wen Xuan* (Selected Literature), fascicle 21. Iritani and Matsumura, 176.

74. *Mr. Zhou*: An ancient successful retailer of juice.

Maozi: 372–289 B.C.E. A Confucian educator of the Warring Period. His deeds and words are collected in *Maozi*. Known for his poverty.

Fangshuo: A meritorious courtier of Emperor Wu (on the throne 140–87 B.C.E.) during the Han Dynasty.

77. *Tao Zhu*: Another name of Fan Li, Warring Period, who served the king of Jue and defeated the king of Wu in 478 B.C.E. Later he lived in Tao (in present-day Shandong Province) and accumulated his wealth.

80. *mulberry*: Its leaves are used for feeding silk worms.

counterweight: That which balances one's deeds on a scale.

82. *outer box*: Made of yellow core cedar to protect the coffin.

84. *Book of Filial Piety*: *Xiao Jing*, a record of a dialogue between Confucius and his student Ceng Shen on filial piety.

88. These quotes are from the Zizhang chapter of *Lunyu* (Dialects). Zizhang and Zijia were young students of Confucius.

89. *six arts*: Ritual, music, archery, horse riding, calligraphy, and algebra.

91. *"Life and death . . ."*: A quotation from *Lunyu* (Dialects).

93. *under the scorching sun*: Literally, in the fifth lunar month, the middle of summer.

95. *hunch back*: Literally "bee waste," a technical term describing a fault of the poetic structure: the second and fourth ideographs of the first column have the same tonal syllable.

skinny legs: Literally "crane knees," a fault like the one above: the fifth ideograph of the first column and the fifth ideograph of the third column have the same tonal syllable.

96. *Lu*: An ancient kingdom (1199–249 B.C.E.), the birthplace of Confucius.

Chaofu: A hermit during the time of Emperor Yao. Yao invited him to ascend to the throne but he declined.

Xuyou: Another legendary hermit at the time of Emperor Yao.

Emperor Yao: A legendary ideal emperor of ancient China.

Emperor Shun: Another legendary ideal emperor of ancient China, succeeding Yao.

98. *Emperor Wu of Han*: On the throne 140–87 B.C.E.

   Emperor Shi of Qin: On the throne 221–210. The founding emperor of the Qin Dynasty.

   golden terrace: Built to enshrine a golden statue of a sorcerer.

   Shaqiu: Where Emperor Shi died while traveling (present-day Hebei Province).

   Moulang: Where Emperor Wu's tomb is located (present-day Shaanxi Province).

   Liqiu: Where Emperor Shi's tomb is located (present-day Shaanxi Province).

101. *East Rock*: Another name for Cold Mountain.

102. *red dust*: In this poem, the term may refer to battles, but it also can mean the dusty world of delusion he left behind.

107. *agada*: Sanskrit, meaning "immortal"—a cure-all medicine.

110. *Yangxiu*: A subject of Cao Cao (founding King Wu) of the Wei Kingdom (155–220). When he saw a coded inscription on a monument, he could immediately decode it.

   wondrous: Two of the ideographs that Yangxiu decoded were the ideographs "young" and "female." Combined, these ideographs make an ideograph that means "wondrous."

111. *five-character-column verses*: The characters are written in vertical columns, the equivalent of the English line. A five-character-column verse means a poem consisting of multiple columns, each made of five characters.

115. *bitter bark*: Yellow bark of Chinese cork trees used for medicine.

117. *mist eater*: Sorcerer.

118. *Hill of Immortals*: Danqiu, one of the peaks of the Mount Tiantai range.

   Mount Siming: An eastern peak of the Mount Tiantai range.

120. *Hill of Immortals*: See note on poem 118.

   Mount Chicheng: Mount "Red Wall," a small mountain standing in the south of Mount Tiantai.

123. *li*: One *li* in the Tang Dynasty was approximately 560 meters (about one-third of a mile).

126. *six sufferings*: Unfortunate short life, sickness, worry, poverty, ugliness, and weakness.

Nine ways to govern: With five elements; with five human activities (facial expression, speech, seeing, listening, and thinking); with eight departments (agricultural, financial, ritual, human service, education, policing, diplomacy, and military); with five natural events (years, months, days, stars, and calendar); with neutrality; with three virtues (honesty, strength, and flexibility); with clear divination; with understanding natural phenomena; and with encouragement and warning.

129. *Three Histories*: Official classics of history: *Shi Ji* (Historical Records); *Han Shu* (Book of Han), and *Houhan Shu* (Book of Later Han).

Five Scriptures: Confucian texts: *Shi Jing* (Book of Odes), *Shu Jing* (Book of Writing), *I Jing* (Book of Change), *Li Ji* (Book of Rites), and *Chunqiu* (Spring and Autumn).

Divination pointed to double unhappiness: In the *I Jing* (Book of Change), this phase of change is described as "Suffering by going, and suffering by coming."

the stars of danger and loss: In ancient astrology, both of these stars, found in a northern constellation, are described as evil.

130. *Who says a sparrow has no horn? It can gouge a hole in a house*: Reference to *Shi Jing* (Book of Odes), a section on Xinglu of Zhaonan.

133. *midsummer*: One of the twenty-four seasons of the year, in the seventh month.

138. *a noisy gourd against a tree*: An ancient legendary hermit, Xuyou, at the time of the mythical Emperor Yao, was given a gourd for drinking, which he hung on a tree. But the sound of the gourd banging against the tree annoyed him so much that he threw it away.

140. *Bo*: Boya, a renowned lute player of the Spring and Autumn Period (770–403 B.C.E.).

Ziqi: Zhong Ziqi, who deeply appreciated Bo's music.

142. *purple mushroom song*: A song about four hermits who lived at the time of the founding emperor of Qin (259–210 B.C.E.). A purple mushroom is believed to be a miraculous herb to make one an immortal.

143. *Huading Peak*: Meaning "Flower Peak." The highest of the Tiantai mountain range, which reaches 3,589 feet.

146. *a fast-running demon*: The demon serving the god of lightning and thunder. His name means "Law" or "Order."

147. *peeled away . . . truth within*: These phrases seem to be related to Zen.

148. *trees of the* saha *world: Saha* is a Sanskrit word that means "endure suffering." Referred to as "stinking cedar." Henricks, 35, note.

149. *Guoqing Monastery*: The main mònastery on Mount Tiantai.
Fenggan: A legendary friend or teacher of Hanshan.
Shide: A legendary friend of Hanshan.
source of water: The "source" here seems to imply dharma companions, and "water" may represent dharma.

151. *My original home*: This seems to refer to Zen.
ren: Six feet.
just so good: Seems to refer to Buddhist sutras where the Buddha praises his followers.

152. *Because the finger points, I see the moon*: Seems to be a reference to a Buddhist metaphor.

153. *boat between shores*: The "boat" means the teaching that helps practitioners journey across the ocean of suffering to the shore of enlightenment.

154. *I've sat steadily*: Seems to refer to Zen.
underground spring: Literally, "Yellow Spring," the world of the deceased.

155. *inexhaustible lamp*: The dharma to be transmitted.

156. *sangha*: Sanskrit, a community of Buddhist practitioners.
mosquito biting an iron ox: This seems to refer to Yaoshan Weiyan (745–828), who heard Mazu Daoyi's words and experienced great enlightenment, saying, "When I was studying with Shitou, it was like a mosquito trying to bite an iron bull."

157. *nimba*: Sanskrit, a tall tree growing in India with bitter flowers, fruit, trunk, and leaves.

158. *Don't be greedy*: Greed, hatred, and ignorance are regarded as elements of basic delusion in Buddhism.

159. *practice intimately:* Seems to refer to Zen.

160. *lotus could bloom in boiling water:* The lotus is a common image of enlightenment in Buddhism.

161. *six paths:* Six worlds of beings in the transmigrating cycle of birth, death, and rebirth: realms of *devas* (gods or celestial beings), human beings, fighting spirits (*asuras*), animals, hungry ghosts, and hell beings.

162. *river of hell:* The river bordering hell. It is said that dead people need to cross one of the three rapids according to their karma.

163. *greedy and randy:* Seems to be a Buddhist phrase.

164. *won't stop eating fish and never gets tired of meat:* Vegetarianism is part of some Buddhist practice.

165. *bodhisattva:* An ideal of Mahayana Buddhism: one who is determined to awaken others before one's own awakening.

166. *demon cave of ignorance:* Both "demon" and "ignorance" are common Buddhist terms.

167. *unwholesome realms:* The lower three of the six paths: realms of hell beings, fighting sprits, and animals.

168. *blind children asking the color of milk:* Reference to the *Pari-nirvana Sutra,* fascicle 14.

169. *hell:* One of the six paths in Buddhist teaching.
    commoner: Literally, the sixth son of the Xu family.

170. *If you buy meat:* See note on poem 164.

171. *white sandalwood:* Used for high quality incense.
    nirvana: Sanskrit, literally, "extinction of fire," meaning extinction of desires, or liberation from the cycle of birth, death, and rebirth.

173. *birth and death:* A common Buddhist phrase.

174. *three talents:* Writing, martial arts, and eloquence.
    six arts: See note on poem 89.
    essence within: Seems to refer to Zen.

175. *river of hell:* See note on poem 162.
    Luer: One of the seven legendary steeds of King Mu (on the throne 1101–946 B.C.E.) of the Zhou Kingdom.

176. *demons: Rakshasa* in Sanskrit. Regarded as eaters of humans.

177. *Southern Court*: The national office for employment, established in 734 in the Bureau of Appointment. Iritani and Matsumura, 167. Henricks, 182, note.

    carrying box: Made of bamboo or wood and carried on the back.

178. *small room*: This may resonate with "Shaoshi (Small Room)" on Mount Song (present-day Henan Province) where Bodhidharma is reputed to have sat in meditation for nine years while facing the wall of a cave.

179. *a raft to cross over*: A way to bring one from the ocean of suffering to the shore of enlightenment.

182. *Diamond Sutra:* One of the *Prajna Paramita* (Realization of Wisdom Beyond Wisdom) scriptures in Mahayana Buddhism.

    bodhisattvas: See note on poem 165.

183. *mugwort grows out of your skull*: Seems to be a Buddhist image.

184. *the Buddha's teaching has twelve parts*: Classifications of the Buddhist scriptures: (1) sutra, a scripture in prose; (2) *geya*, a teaching reiterated in verse; (3) *vyakarana*, a prediction of enlightenment; (4) *gatha*, a verse for chanting; (5) *udana*, a teaching expounded not in response to a question; (6) *nidana*, an explanation of causes of unwholesome things; (7) *avadana*, a parable; (8) *itivrittaka*, a past life of a disciple of the Buddha; (9) *jataka*, a past life of the Buddha; (10) *vaipulya*, a broad teaching; (11) *adbhuta-dharma*, an unprecedented (magical) story; (12) *upadesha*, a philosophical discussion.

    lion's roar: Teaching of the Buddha.

185. *naked insect*: A human being.

    scriptures of Dao and De: The two volumes of the *Daode Jing* attributed to Laozi. *Dao* means the "way," and *De* means "virtue" or "power."

    sword of wisdom: A common Buddhist phrase.

186. *red braided cord*: A sign of a high official.

    like a hunter who wears a monk's robe: Reference to the *Pari-nirvana Sutra*, fascicle 7.

187. *ferry*: See note on poem 153.

188. *Lute Valley*: An upper stream of the River Han (present-day Shaanxi Province).

Parrot Island: A sandbank in the River Chang (present-day Hebei Province).

189. *stupa*: Sanskrit, Buddhist tower, originally where the Buddha's relics were enshrined.

190. *transmigration*: A Vedic, Hindu, and Buddhist concept.

191. *Three Rapid River*: See note on poem 162.

192. *"Since birth..."*: Laozi, fascicle 80.

ladder to the clouds: A very tall ladder for entering an enemy's castle.

193. *karma*: Sanskrit, "action." Also a visible and invisible result of action.

194. *sentient beings:* A common Buddhist phrase.

196. *its original nature*: A Buddhist concept.

197. *five skandhas:* Five streams of body and mind: form (body), perception, feeling, inclination, and discernment. *Skandha* is a Sanskrit word that means "heap," "aggregates," or "path."

198. *ten thousand phenomena*: All things.

wish-granting jewel: Sanskrit, *mani*.

199. *six paths*: See note on poem 161.

200. *Southern Continent*: According to sutras, the world consists of eight seas among nine mountains that lie around Mount Sumeru. Among the four continents that lie in the eight seas, the Southern Continent, Jambudvipa, is where we humans live with suffering, but where there is the potential for awakening.

three poisons: Greed, hatred, and ignorance.

201. *that one thing*: An inexhaustible lamp. See note on poem 155.

202. *number*: A number indicating the birth order of siblings, for example, Second Son of Wang.

true mind, solid as a diamond: A common Mahayana Buddhist analogy.

205. *mugwort door*: A humble door.

never seen cranes become immortals: A white crane is a Daoist symbol of immortality.

206. *evil birds*: The delusions of view and fundamental ignorance. Two-headed birds appear in the *Samyuktaratnapitaka Sutra* and *Abhinishkramana Sutra*. Red Pine, 188, note.

three poisonous snakes: See note on poem 200.

207. *ordinary way of living*: This seems to refer to the words of Nanquan Puyuan (748–834) "Ordinary mind is the way."

208. *sit upright*: A common Zen phrase.

209. *three realms*: Roughly meaning the entire world of phenomena and beyond: (1) desire realm, including the six paths (see note on poem 161); (2) form realm of those who are free from desire; (3) formless realm of those who have attained the highest worldly mental states through meditative exercises.

six paths: See note on poem 161.

talk to each other like wood to stone: Talking without communicating.

210. *delusion*: A common Buddhist term.

211. *six brothers*: Six-sense organs.

one [of them]: Mind.

bodhisattva: See note on poem 165.

all three mountains: Body, speech, thought.

212. *from earlier karma*: Result of action from a past life. A common Buddhist concept.

213. *Let me say to those who eat meat*: See note on poem 164.

214. *Transmigration over eons*: See note on poem 161.

215. *burning house*: A parable in the *Lotus Sutra*. To rescue children playing in a house on fire, someone told them about three carts pulled by sheep, deer, and an ox outside the house.

three carts: From the same parable.

ten directions: North, south, east, west, their midpoints, plus up and down.

216. *eight calendar points*: Beginning of spring, spring equinox, beginning of summer, summer solstice, beginning of autumn, autumn equinox, beginning of winter, and winter solstice.

Ride the white ox into an open field: See note on poem 215.

217. *person of ease*: A person of nondoing—a Zen concept.

218. *If you take their hide and meat*: See note on poem 164.

219. *lotus comes out of the muddy water*: A common Buddhist phrase regarding enlightenment.

221. *Yama*: The king of hell.

Three Rapid River: See note on poem 162.

treasure inside your own robe: A parable in the *Lotus Sutra*: A man went to see a dear friend, got drunk, and fell asleep. The friend, who was going on a long, official journey, sewed a priceless pearl inside his robe as a gift, but the man never noticed it.

222. *Cold Spring*: We agree with Red Pine: "Apparently, Han Quan (Cold Spring) was the name Cold Mountain gave to the stream that was visible from his cave." Red Pine, 238, note.

not Zen: Zen beyond Zen.

223. *no worries*: No delusions, a common Buddhist concept.

224. *empty your mind*: Seems to refer to Zen.

225. *eight winds*: Pleasure and pain, praise and blame, fame and disrepute, gain and loss.

peaceful dwelling: A three-month summer practice period in the Zen tradition. This poem may have a loose reference to the term.

Tiger Hill: Huqiu—an ancient spiritual mountain in the Su Region (present-day Jiangsu Province).

Tiger Valley: Huxi—also an ancient spiritual place in Lushan (present-day Jiangxi Province)

Lord Zhou: See note on poem 66.

Shao: Who assisted Lord Zhou (see above note) in the early Zhou period. His name should also be spelled Zhou, but to avoid confusion, we spell it Shao.

226. *Zhou's commentary*: A treatise on the *Shi Jing* (Book of Odes) by Zhou Xuan (127–200) of the Later Han Dynasty.

Mao's interpretation: A commentary on the *Shi Jing* (Book of Odes) by Mao Heng and Mao Chang of the Early Han Dynasty (206 B.C.E.– 7 C.E.).

clear-eyed people: Seems to refer to Zen.

227. *five betrayals*: These are (1) to kill the mother, (2) to kill the father, (3) to kill an arhat, (4) to injure the Buddha and cause to bleed, (5) to destroy the harmony of the Buddhist community.

ten unwholesome actions: Actions prohibited by precepts: (1) to kill, (2) to steal, (3) to misuse sex, (4) to make false statements, (5) to sell alcohol, (6) to discuss the faults of other home-leaver bodhisattvas (7) to praise yourself and insult others, (8) to withhold dharma or treasure, (9) to be angry, (10) to slander the three treasures.

228. *wish-granting jewel*: See note on poem 198.

232. *Mount Sumeru*: See note on poem 200.

234. *Dipankara Buddha*: A mythical teacher of Shakyamuni Buddha.

tathagata: Sanskrit, literally, "one who has thus gone; one who has thus come; or one who has come from thusness." An honorific of a buddha.

238. *Sengyao*: Zhang Sengyao, a well-known painter of the Liang Dynasty.

Liang Dynasty: Southern Kingdom, 502–556.

Daozi: Daozi Wu, a painter at the time of Emperor Xuan (685–762) of the Tang Dynasty.

Master Zhi: Baozhi, 479–514, a renowned monk of the Liang Dynasty. Known as a practitioner of magic, he looked so compassionate and at the same time so fierce that—according to *Fozu Gangmu* (Gazette of Buddha Ancestors), published in 1634—Sengyao could not paint his portrait.

239. *green-feathered hair ornament*: The female kingfisher feather is green, while the male feather is red.

240. *dusty world*: A world full of desire and delusion.

241. *Cold Cliff*: Hanyuan, the name of Hanshan's abode.

245. *seven treasures*: Gold, silver, lapis lazuli, moonstone, agate, coral, and amber. (The list varies according to the sutras.)

248. *Hanyuan*: See note on poem 241.

249. The source of this poem is Ota, 238.

251. *three realms*: See note on poem 209.

four types of birth: Birth by egg, womb, moisture, or transformation.

255. *purple mushrooms*: Medicine in sorcery.

259. *three unwholesome paths*: See note on poem 167.

261. *Mount Vipula*: Sanskrit, meaning a very high mountain.

262. *jade tree*: A tree made of jade that produces fruit of jade, believed to be a tree of the immortals.

264. *Yunxiaguan Temple*: Meaning "Cloud Mist View."

while waiting for the white crane to arrive: Daoist immortals were believed to have magical abilities to transform people into cranes in order to fly on various journeys.

265. *three carts*: See note on poem 215.

266. *hosts . . . guests*: The host means to be a true person or a teacher; the guest is someone still searching or a student.

267. *kingdom of Liang*: Kingdom in the south (502–556).

Baozhi: He (418–514) taught Emperor Wu, the founding monarch of Liang.

Wanhui: A monk of the Tang Dynasty. Also named Fayun. Possibly Hanshan meant to refer to Fayun of Guangzhai Monastery, Liang Dynasty (467–529). Iritani and Matsumura, 240.

four sorcerers: Daoists who practiced Buddhism: Zhenbai, Qing Xupei, Tongbai, and Ziyang Zhou.

Bodhisattva (Layman) Fu: One (497–569) who lectured Emperor Wu on the *Diamond Sutra*.

Tathagatha: See note on poem 234.

This poem describes Hanshan's understanding of southern China when Bodhidharma arrived from India.

271. *Vedic scripture*: The sacred text of Veda, the ancient Indian religion.

Three Teachings: Daoism, Confucianism, and Buddhism.

276. *Mount Vipula*: See note on poem 261.

277. *three realms*: See note on poem 209.

wood lice: Burdock seeds that stick to the mouth and hair, and are hard to remove.

286. *Don't blame others for their faults*: Confucius's words in the "Lunyu" (*Analects*) section on Yanyuan.

287. *polishing a rough tile*: This is based on the following interaction: Mazu Daoyi (709–788) said, "I intend to become a buddha." Then his teacher, Nanyue Huairang (677–744), picked up a tile and started

polishing it on a stone near Mazu's hut. Mazu said, "Master, what are you doing?" Nanyue said, "Polishing a tile." Mazu said, "Why are you polishing the tile?" Nanyue said, "I am trying to make a mirror." Mazu said, "How can you polish a tile and make a mirror?" Nanyue said, "How can you do zazen and become a buddha?"

291. For the source of this poem, see page 242 in "A Study of the Poet."

293. *five skandhas*: See note on poem 197.

   four snakes: Four great elements in ancient Indian classification: earth, water, fire, and air.

   three poisons: See note on poem 200.

   six thieves: Six-sense consciousness: eye consciousness, ear consciousness, nose consciousness, tongue consciousness, skin consciousness, and mind consciousness.

294. *Five Mountains*: Renowned mountains of China: Tai (east), Hua (west), Heng (south), Heng (north), and Song (center).

   Sumeru: See note on poem 200.

   ten entanglements: Ten types of delusion—shamelessness, remorselessness, jealousy, avarice, regret, straying, lamenting, depression, anger, and upset.

295. *Shi Qinu*: A wealthy man in the kingdom of West Jin (c. 1100–c. 770 B.C.E.). He was killed in a fight over his beautiful mistress, Luzhu.

296. *realm beyond nonthinking*: The highest realm of the devas or heavenly beings.

297. *six thieves*: See note on poem 293.

   pearl sewn in the back of a robe: See note on poem 221.

299. *arhat*: A disciple of the Buddha.

   Yunguang: A monk at the time of Emperor Wu of the kingdom of Liang, who was good at preaching but broke the precepts, so it is said he was reborn as a cow.

301. *a blue-eyed stranger*: Blue-eyed foreigners, especially Persians, were believed to have the mysterious ability to find treasures. Iritani and Matsumura, 335

302. *patched robes*: Worn over one shoulder by a Buddhist monk or nun.

303. *Maitreya*: The future buddha, predicted to come down from Tushita Heaven to the continent of Jambudvipa 5,670,000,000 years in the future as the next buddha. Will awaken those who have missed the teaching of Shakyamuni Buddha.

306. *wheel-turning king*: The Buddha, who turns the wheel of dharma.

    ten types of virtue: Not to kill, not to steal, not to have unwholesome sex, not to lie, not to contradict, not to speak ill, not to speak fictitiously, not to be greedy, not to resent, and not to express a crooked view.

    seven treasures: See note on poem 245.

    six paths: See note on poem 161.

307. *turning sutras*: Reading Buddhist scriptures.

    entanglements: State of mind, such as delusion, that takes over. See note on poem 294 ("ten entanglements").

310. *ten names*: Ten honorifics of Shakyamuni Buddha: Worthy of Offering, True Encompassing Knower, Clear Walker, Well Gone, Knower of the World, Unsurpassable Warrior, Excellent Tamer, Teacher of Humans and Devas, Buddha, the World-Honored One.

    "Good Guide": Implying a buddha.

312. *flowers in the sky*: Also can be translated as "flowers of emptiness."

Map of China

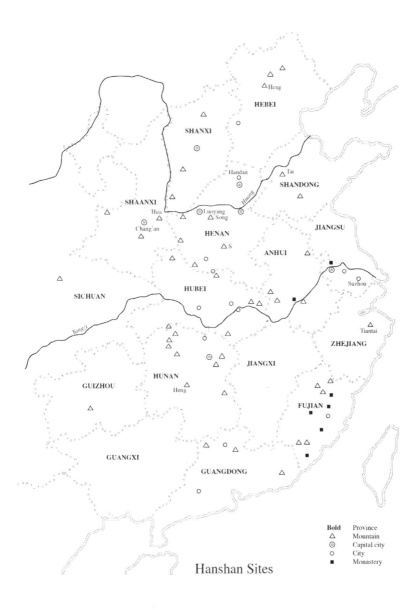

HEBEI

△
△
△ Heng

SHANXI
△
◎
○

Handan
○
SHANDONG
△ Tai
△

SHAANXI
Hua
Chang'an
△
Luoyang ◎
△ Song
Huang
○
△

HENAN
△ S
△
○
△
△

ANHUI
○
◎ ○
Suzhou

JIANGSU

HUBEI
△
△
△
△
△ Yang'zi
△
△
△

JIANGXI
◎
△

ZHEJIANG
△ Tiantai
■
■

GUIZHOU
△

HUNAN
Heng
△
△

GUANGXI

GUANGDONG
△ ○
△
△ △
△

FUJIAN
△ △
■
○
■
■

Bold   Province
△   Mountain
◎   Capital city
○   City
■   Monastery

Hanshan Sites

Record of the Hanshan Anthology

L U Q I U   Y I N , *Imperial Counsel, Military Commander of Tai Region, Recipient of an Imperial Scarlet Bag*

As far as I understand, no one knows who Hanshan is. People, including aged ones, regard him as a poor crazy man. He secludes himself about seventy *li* west of the Tangxing Prefecture of Tiantai. Calling himself Hanyuan, he lives there and at times returns to Guoqing Monastery.

In this monastery, there is a man named Shide who works in the kitchen and keeps leftover vegetables in a bamboo pipe. When Hanshan comes, he sends the bamboo pipe off with Hanshan carrying it on his back. Sometimes Hanshan walks in a hallway and screams with joy, talking and smiling to himself. When a monk catches and beats him, uttering slanderous words, Hanshan stands clapping his hands in laughter and leaves after a while. He looks poor and exhausted. Every word of his speech, however, makes sense, and if we think deeply, it inspires our heart about the way. Whenever he utters words, they express profound stillness.

He wears a birch-bark hat and torn clothes and walks in wooden clogs. This is how a master conceals his achievement, identifying with others to guide them. At times he walks in a long hallway, shouting, "Yah, yeah, the three realms transmigrate." At another time, he goes to a village, singing and laughing with children of cow herders. He argues or agrees with them and enjoys their company. Who, other than a deep thinker, can understand his true nature?

I was appointed to be governor of Tangxing Province, and on my way to take the job, I was struck with a heavy headache. I saw an *I Jing* practitioner, and a doctor attended me, but the illness got worse.

That was when I met Zen Master Fenggan, who told me that he had come from Guoqing Monastery, on Mount Tiantai, to meet me. So I asked him to cure my illness. Smiling, he said, "Our body consists of the four great elements, and illness arises from illusion. If you want to remove it, you should use pure water." So I brought pure water to him. He sprayed it on me, and my headache immediately was gone. Then he said, "The Tai Region has poisonous storms from the ocean. You should take care of yourself when you get there."

I said to Fenggan, "I wonder if there is someone who can be my teacher." He replied, "If you see, you don't know. If you know, you don't see. If you want to see, do not be concerned with the shape but just see. Hanshan is Manjushri Bodhisattva and hides in Guoqing. Shide is Samantabhadra Bodhisattva, who looks poor and acts crazy. He comes and goes to its kitchen, moves around and tends the fire." Having said this, he bid farewell and left.

Proceeding on my journey, I got to my office in Tai Region but did not forget Fenggan's words. On the third day of my job, I went up to a Zen monastery and asked a monk there about what Fenggan had said. Everything coincided with his words. So I asked an official of Tangxing Province to find the whereabouts of Hanshan and Shide. After a while I received a report: About seventy *li* from the border of the province, there was a cave. An old man noticed a poor man living in the cave who often visited the Guoqing Monastery, where he stayed in the kitchen, and where there was a worker named Shide.

So I went to the Guoqing Monastery, bowed to the Buddha, and asked a monk there about Zen Master Fenggan's temple and if he had seen Hanshan and Shide.

The monk said, "Zen Master Fenggan's temple is in the back of the sutra storehouse. At this time nobody is there except for a tiger, who is often there and roars. Both Hanshan and Shide are in the kitchen." He brought me to the temple. When we opened it, it only had traces of a tiger.

I said, "What does Zen Master Fenggan do when he is here?"

The monk said, "He pounds rice and offers it to the assembly of monks. At night he enjoys himself singing."

When we got to the kitchen, we saw two men greatly laughing in front of the oven. I bowed to them. One after another they yelled at me, taking each other's hand, and said laughing, "Fenggan speaks too much. Without knowing Amitabha Buddha, what's the use of bowing to us?"

Surprised monks rushed to us and said, "Why do you bow to these poor guys, sir?"

The two men held each other's hand and ran out of the monastery. I asked the monks to catch them, but Hanshan and Shide went away to Hanyuan Cave.

I asked the monks who were chasing Hanshan and Shide if they would come back to the monastery. Then I made an arrangement to have a room ready for them in case they came back. After returning to town, I had two sets of clean robes sewn and sent them, together with incense and medicine, to Hanshan and Shide. But the messenger found out that they had not come back to the monastery. So he brought my gifts to Hanyuan Cave.

Hanshan saw the messenger and yelled out, "Thief, thief!" He returned to his cave and said, "You guys, endeavor, endeavor."

Then he disappeared into the cave. The opening of the cave closed itself, and there was no way for the messenger to follow him. There was no trace of Shide.

Later, I asked the monk Daoqiao to find out about the past behavior of Hanshan. Daoqiao assembled over three hundred poems Hanshan had written on bamboo, wood, stones, and walls of village houses and offices, as well as poems Shide had written on shrine walls. Thus, he compiled this volume. Because I had put my heart in Buddha's teaching, I was fortunate enough to meet these practitioners of the way.

Here is my verse of admiration:

Fleeing from the bodhisattva path
he became a poor man.

Living alone on Cold Mountain
he enjoys his pursuit.
His appearance is withered
his clothes are tattered.
He speaks and writes verses
truthful and profound.
Ordinary people lack appreciation
and call him crazy.
Once he got to Tiantai
and entered Guoqing Monastery.
He slowly walks on a long hallway
laughing and snapping his fingers.
At times he runs and stands
chattering to himself.
When eating at the kitchen
he only receives leftover vegetables.
When he wrote a sad poem
monks and laypeople yelled and beat him.
He was serene
and people were ashamed.
His movements were free
and difficult to understand by ordinary people.
But by uttering one word
he immediately removed their worldly entanglement.
Once at Guoqing Monastery
he copied iconographic drawings
offered them to the Buddha
and became a disciple.
In the past he lived in Hanshan
and came to this place.
I bow to Manjushri
who is Cold Mountain.
I take refuge in Samantabhadra

who is no other than Shide.
Expressing my admiration
I wish to go beyond birth and death.

A Study of the Poet

Kazuaki Tanahashi

A Marvel of Poetry and Legend

Hanshan's poems are highly revered in the Zen tradition. Hakuin Ekaku (1686–1768)—regarded as the restorer of the Rinzai School, one of the two major streams of Zen Buddhism in Japan—saw in Hanshan an ideal among meditation practitioners. Hakuin's three-fascicle commentary on Hanshan's poetry is titled *Kanzan Shi Sendai Kimon* (Icchantica's Notes on the Hanshan Poems).[1] (A fascicle is a chapter-long text bound independently. *Icchantica* in Sanskrit means one who can never be enlightened—an ironic title.) Hakuin is often direct but sometimes sets in motion over three thousand words to elucidate one poem.[2]

Hakuin characterizes one of the Hanshan poems as expressing "an extremely profound aspect of mountain dwelling in retreat with high leisure."[3] Of another he says, "This is a barrier guarded by nine tigers [impossible to penetrate]."[4] And of another, "This has the most subtle secret of the Hanshan poems. If you students peruse it and clap your hands, all the steep hills in this anthology will suddenly melt like ice."[5]

Hakuin's commentary appears in the third of four Japanese commentaries on the Hanshan poems in the Edo Period (1603–1867)—all written by Zen monks.[6] Strikingly, there is no existing Chinese commentary on the Hanshan poems from the premodern period. One record, however, notes that Caoshan Benji (840–901), regarded as a cofounder of the Caodong School of Zen in China, wrote a seven-fascicle commentary on the Hanshan poems, but the text is not extant, and there is no other cross-reference to prove that Caoshan actually wrote such a commentary.[7]

217

There is a legend that the great Chinese poet Du Fu (712–770) took a glance at a Hanshan poem and "tied his tongue" (meaning that he shut up).[8] Later, Huang Shangu (1045–1105), another renowned poet and calligrapher, was asked by his Zen master, Hutang Baojue (1025–1100), to compose a poem after Hanshan; Shangu tried as much as he could but was unable to get a phrase. He confessed to Baojue: "Even if I read and try to compose for ten more years, or in my next lifetime, I won't be able to write like Hanshan." Baojue understood him.[9] Much later, in 1707, the Hanshan anthology was included in an imperial collection of the Qin Dynasty, the *Quan Tang Shi* (Entire Tang Dynasty Poetry), which consists of nine hundred fascicles encompassing 49,000 poems by more than 2,200 poets.

Hanshan and his companion Shide have been portrayed in paintings since the Song Dynasty (960–1278) in China. In Japan, when Zen culture began to flourish after the Muromachi Period (1336–1573), Hanshan poetry and legend captured the imagination of Zen painters so that portraits of these two hermits became one of their favorite themes. I only know of a few paintings where Hanshan has been portrayed alone. Rather, in most cases, he has been paired with his symbiotic half, Shide, who represents nonintellectual work and the practice of Zen. Such a dual format seems to be a unique form of figure paintings. These hermits are usually portrayed with shaggy hair but well-shaven faces, long fingernails, and tattered robes, while exposing exaggerated grins. Hanshan often carries a brush and a roll of paper, or occasionally writes a poem on a standing tree, and Shide holds a broom. The paintings may have mountains with ragged rocks in the background, or the figures may be just floating in empty space.

Through the centuries, painters seemed engaged in a competition to conjure ever more mystical images of these mountain figures. The pair would eventually come to be depicted with resoundingly grotesque smiles, as in this depiction by Sansetsu Kano (1589–1651; see illustration),

from the collection of Shinsho Gokuraku Temple—Shinnyo-do, Kyoto. Some paintings also portrayed these two hermits together with their presumed teacher Fenggan, who is sitting on a tiger.

Ironically, some of these ancient depictions of Hanshan and Shide, who lived simple lives in poverty with almost nothing in their possession, are rated as national treasures and housed in reputable museums.[10]

Japan has a millennium and a half of scholarship on Chinese literature. It is in this tradition, following Zen monks' commentaries, that Teizo Ota published 312 Hanshan poems in 1934 in their original Chinese and the Japanese way of reading Chinese, with annotations.[11] His work has become the standard Japanese anthology of Hanshan. In 1958, Yoshitaka Iriya, also an accomplished scholar of Chinese literature, published a pioneering study of Hanshan and his poems, including his Japanese translation of an annotation of 108 poems.[12] We can also rely upon the scholarship of Sensuke Iritani and Takashi Matsumura as presented in *Kanzan Shi* (Hanshan Poems), published in 1970. A great many other publications on Hanshan have been produced along with these scholars' works. There is even one waterproof book with a title that can be translated as "Hanshan Poems for Your Bath Time."

Arthur Waley, a renowned British expert on Oriental studies, first translated Hanshan into English with his simply titled book *27 Poems by Han-shan*. In his 1954 publication, he said: "Cold Mountain is often the name of a state of mind rather than a locality. It is on this conception, as well as on that of the 'hidden treasure,' the Buddha who is to be sought not somewhere outside us, but 'at home' in the heart, that the mysticism of the poems is based."[13]

Jack Kerouac dedicated his book *The Dharma Bums* to Hanshan in 1958. In this novel Kerouac describes the translation process of Hanshan by Jaffy Ryder, who is a fictional portrayal of the American poet Gary Snyder. Jaffy explains why Hanshan is his hero:

> Because he was a poet, a mountain man, a Buddhist dedicated to the principle of meditation on the essence of all things, a vegetarian too by the way though I haven't got on that kick from figuring maybe in this modern world to be a vegetarian is to split hairs a little since all sentient beings eat what they can. And he was a man of solitude who could take off by himself and live purely and true to himself.[14]

At the age of twenty-eight, Gary Snyder, who later became one of the greatest poets of our time, published his translation of twenty-four Hanshan poems in his book *Cold Mountain* in 1958. These translations ignited a great appreciation of Hanshan within the counterculture of the times and beyond in the Western world.

Burton Watson, another outstanding translator, published *Cold Mountain: 100 Poems by the T'ang Poet Han-Shan* in 1962.

We are also blessed by the works of Red Pine, who, in *The Collected Songs of Cold Mountain*, translated 307 Hanshan poems into English, presenting them along with their Chinese originals, in 1984.

The Poetry of Han-Shan, the English translation of 311 Hanshan poems by Robert G. Henricks with detailed scholarly annotations, published in 1990, also benefits us greatly.

Seclusion in a Sacred Mountain

Many spiritual seekers fantasize about living alone on a mountain in pursuit of sublime freedom and timeless insight. Yet, we know it would be grossly inconvenient and nearly impossible to carry out in our lifetime. So we bow to hermits who may be carrying out their retreat on our behalf. This is especially true if the hermits share with us poems describing their experience and findings, whether it is loneliness, longing, despair, or joy—we love it all. That's why Hanshan has been a teacher and idol for many throughout the generations.

Hanshan, or "Cold Mountain," is what he calls himself. It's the place where he lives. But also, as Burton Watson points out, it's a state of mind. And it's a state of his spiritual experience. The hermit also calls himself Hanyuan—"Cold Rock" or "Cold Cliff"—after his abode, the cave. In the Tiantai area in southeastern China, there still exists a place called Hanyuan, where there is a large cave in which it is believed that he lived.

Reading through his verses, we glimpse his life on Cold Mountain: The narrow path to his cave from villages and towns covers a great distance, and there's no trace of horse or cart. Under layers of peaks, he goes through switchbacks of the valley road, wet with lush grass, where boulders are stacked. He climbs up the mountainside while grabbing vines on an ivy-covered path and climbs down with an old wisteria cane.

Winter comes early on this mountain, with the occasional roaring of storms and dense snowfalls. Even in summer the sun remains hidden in the mist morning after morning and the ice does not melt. In the daytime, the steaming clouds do not drift away, making the poet wonder if it has been chilly since ancient times. There are pine trees all over the high cliffs. Bamboo stalks in the groves are tall and dark, where the constant weeping of the valley stream rises from underneath. Monkeys pluck the wild fruit and cry out. Tigers and deer are the poet's neighbors. The sound of birds speaking is at times too sad to bear, while bees and butterflies express their joy. The "layers of mountains and rivers are exquisite," and the poet adores their utter beauty.

Hanshan's abode is a gloomy cave under the green mossy rock. He has perhaps built a door woven with mugwort stems to shelter against the cold and to protect himself from beasts. The floor may be covered with pine needles, and his bed is made of soft, thin grass. He has a small garden, which may be overgrown with weeds. He wears a humble dull-color leather-and-cloth garment as a jacket in summer and as a quilt in winter. He wears a birch-bark hat and perhaps a self-made pair of shoes for treading on pebbles and rocks. A straw raincoat shelters him from rain or snow.

The hermit draws water from a brook. He carries his basket to collect mountain greens, fruit, and nuts. He gathers fern sprouts to sustain him through the year. When cold comes, he makes a small fire. When hunger comes, he lays out vegetables on a reed mat and boils them together in a thin soup on the fire pit. To nurture his thin body, he eats from his gourd bowl with chopsticks made of twigs. On the ground of his cave, medicine simmers in a clay pot; he keeps jars of yellow pine pollen, cypress bud tea, and fragrant gel.

He says he has no possessions and is confident that nobody will take the trouble to climb up to his cave to steal something. But, I assume, he must collect firewood to get though the severe winters, as well as have a pair of flint stones, a knife, and likely a broom made of grass. Also he needs a brush, an ink stick, and some paper, although he occasionally writes his poems on a stone wall inside or outside his cave.

Sitting on a grass mat laid out on flat ground or an uneven stone, leaning against a boulder in contemplation or idle thinking are the main parts of Hanshan's daily routine. When the moon is full, he may sit out for a long time. He reads and writes. He sings alone, while circumambulating the mountain or climbing to the top of a peak.

Hanshan wishes to stay obscure and be free from the stain of worldly affairs. Yet he is lonely with the thought that there is no one around him. He has a strong longing for a way-seeking friend with whom he could discuss in depth life, poetry, and spiritual practice. Most friends are already dead, but once in a long while he has a visitor. He sometimes walks to the Guoqing Monastery near the plain to see Shide and Fenggan—friends but perhaps not his teachers. Monks at the monastery say that Hanshan is a fool. But he doesn't mind, having the conviction that they are the ignorant ones, not him.

Space, Time, and Belief

The mountains of Tiantai ("Heavenly Terrace") that embrace Hanshan's Cold Rock cave uphold a long chain of peaks. Its range runs from west to east of Zhejiang Province, to Hanzhou Bay on the East China Sea. The mountains are rocky and known for their magical beauty. From ancient times this area has been believed to be the home of many spirits and immortals, where Daoist adepts have taken refuge.

Being a lone dweller on a mountain, Hanshan follows the path of Daoism in its extremity: no activity as ultimate activity, being in accord with the flow of nature with ease, freedom from care, and the joy of quietude. He reads the Daoist base text, *Daode Jing* (Virtue of the Way), attributed to Laozi, which is full of paradox and enigma. He uses sorcerers' herbs for healing and longevity and fantasizes engaging in the practice of becoming an immortal, which only results in disappointment and doubt.

The first Buddhist community on Tiantai was founded in the third century. Later, the monk Zhiyi (538–597) settled there and was honored by Emperor Wen of the Sui Dynasty, who had reunited China in 589 after many centuries of fracture. A brilliant Buddhist theologian, Zhiyi classified a great number of scriptures, containing varied and sometimes contradictory teachings of Shakyamuni Buddha, into five categories, which presumably the Buddha had given to people in different stages of their maturity. Zhiyi placed the *Lotus Sutra* at the end. He encouraged his students to deepen their intellectual studies and engage in the practice of meditation and rituals. His posthumous name was Great Master Tiantai, and his main monastery on Tiantai was named Guoqing ("Purifier of the Nation") soon after his death. His eclectic institution was called the Tiantai School. The mountains he dwelled in became the site of one of the greatest Buddhist universities of China. Many prominent students visited Tiantai, including the Japanese monk Saicho, who practiced there in 804, and upon returning home established its Japanese form, the Tendai School. During its prime, Mount Tiantai housed seventy-two major temples, as well as innumerable shrines and hermitages.

Hanshan must have been familiar with the extensive array of temples on the mountain and the highly institutionalized practice of Buddhism in its center, the Guoqing Monastery. He mentions in a poem the name of this monastery, but he keeps his silence as if he does not see Buddhist images or a great many monks participating in strictly scheduled daily routines. It's possible that he goes to see his friends only on their free days. But how does he not mention the magnificence of the buildings, library, landscape gardens, statues, and art?

The school of Zen (Chan in Chinese, which came from the Sanskrit word *dhyana*, meaning meditation) advocates intense, continuous meditation that results in transcending intellectual understanding and reaching a direct individual experience of nondualistic insight. Begun with a small number of teachers and students in sixth-century China, it has formed lineages of highly systematized and ritualized monastic institutions since the time of Dajian Huineng (638–713), who is regarded as the founder of the Southern School of Zen, which emphasized sudden enlightenment. Stories of paradoxical dialogues between students and teachers, and their peculiar behaviors, began to be recorded around the time of Mazu Daoyi (709–788). These anecdotes, particularly from the eighth to mid-tenth centuries during the formation of the Five Schools of Zen, were studied and pondered upon by later practitioners. In many cases such ancient stories were even more revered and investigated than scriptures of Indian origin as clues to leap into the ultimate truth. Thus, Zen may be seen as a branch of Mahayana Buddhism from India shaped by the Chinese Daoist paradigm.

Some of Hanshan's poems demonstrate his close association with Zen. One of his poems speaks about having left the household.[15] This phrase usually means becoming a monk or nun, but also it can be interpreted as merely renouncing family and social life. He may or may not have undergone formal monastic training. We don't see any indication in his poems that in his cave he had a Buddhist image, robe, or Daoist talisman. Although he says he possesses nothing, it is possible that he kept volumes of Zen books and a copy of the *Pari-nirvana Sutra* and the *Lotus Sutra*, along with the *Daode Jing*.

In the sixth and seventh centuries, China, from a secular point of view, was a world empire with a highly developed civilization. The unified empire of Sui, based in Luoyang, went into decline when Emperor Yang ascended to the throne in 605 as its second monarch. Yang was an atrocious tyrant whose corrupt rule pressed his subjects with high taxation and induced a revolt of farmers all over China. Foreseeing a collapse of the Sui Dynasty, a young man named Li Shimin (599–649) urged his father— the grand lord Li Yuan (566–635)—to raise an army against the emperor. The young Shimin successfully led diplomatic and military campaigns, abolished the Sui Dynasty in 617, and initiated the Tang Dynasty in 618, installing his father as the founding emperor. After pacifying revolts and surviving his jealous brothers' attempt to kill him, Shimin asked his father to retire; thus he became the second emperor, Tai, of the Tang Dynasty in 626 at age twenty-eight. He succeeded in swallowing neighboring states in northern and central Asia, subordinating southern nations, and making China's domain larger than ever. In 645 he asked Xuanzhan, who had studied in India and recently brought home a great number of Sanskrit scriptures, to lead a national translation project. Xuanzhan's accurate and extensive translation work helped deepen scholarship, which resulted in a golden age of Buddhism all over East Asia.

The capital city Chang'an, situated on the southern bank of the River Wei in the Guanzhong basin (present-day Shaanxi Province), was an orderly gridded megalopolis, guarded by massive dirt walls. By the first part of the eighth century, this powerful capital city had a population of more than one million people, as well as a prospering culture and commerce. The society, however, was rigidly hierarchical and discriminatory against women and the uneducated, as Confucian values remained the basis of conduct in society.

Emperor Tai perfected a civil service examination system for hiring different levels of government officials, open to anyone of any background—a system that had been initiated by Emperor Wen, the first monarch of the Sui Dynasty. All men who were educated members of society, except those who were members of the aristocracy, must have dreamed about passing the extremely demanding examination and being appointed to a civil position, receiving high prestige and salary. Of course the great majority of them did not make it. Some recognized poets from this time, including Li Bo (701–762) and Du Fu (712–770), were also failed applicants.

One can easily imagine that Hanshan was no exception and harbored such a fantasy of getting selected to be a public servant. We don't know if he did try or succeed. At least he had an affinity with failed scholars, as we see in poem 76.

Current Hanshan Sites

A cave where Hanshan is believed to have lived is in a village called Hanyuan ("Cold Rock") near the city of Jietou, twenty-one miles west of the Guoqing Monastery at the foot of Mount Tiantai. To visit this cave and other sites related to Hanshan (as well as sites prominent in the life of the Japanese Zen Master Dogen), Peter Levitt and I led a pilgrimage to Zhejiang Province, China, in spring 2017. A dozen of us (representing six nationalities, including a Chinese guide) stayed in a hotel that was walking distance from the Guoqing Monastery. A microbus took us on a freeway past farms and orchards to the foot of a hill with a widespread washed-brown granite cliff. We climbed on a narrow path for ten minutes to the bottom of the cliff, where there was a giant half-round open cave that could easily contain a single-story house.[16] We saw no other visitors, but someone seemed to be living in a poorly built shed on one side of the cave close to the entrance. A small altar had been placed in the center, and at its side a woman had a tableful of incense and talismans to sell.

The local government advertises this cave as the ancient Hanshan abode. It is possible that our poet stayed there for a while. But, to me, the extra-wide opening of this cave would clearly have offered little to no protection from wild creatures. In addition, the site is located close to the flat area of the region and doesn't match Hanshan's description of an abode far away from human traces. I would argue that he must have lived in a deeper and higher part of the Tiantai mountain range.

After spending some time in and out of the cave, we visited a nearby Hanshan Mingyuan Temple, which was situated on the same level as the farmland but backed with a high cliff of numerous giant, gray boulders with a very tall waterfall. Similar to the majority of Buddhist temples in China, this sanctuary had been destroyed during the Cultural Revolution that raged throughout the nation between 1966 and 1976. But a number of medium-size and small halls to fill the seven caves of the temple had been rebuilt recreating a serene, authentic ambiance. Also, the construction of large guest quarters was almost complete. Huixian, the abbess of this nunnery, which presently houses three nuns, warmly welcomed us, the pilgrims, and shared with us the Hanshan legend of this place: Hanshan was being pursued by men on horseback and escaped to the bottom of the cliff, when some boulders moved to block his pursuers. Later this temple was built to commemorate that event.

There is another temple named after our poet—the renowned Hanshan Temple in Suzhou, the city known for its scenic canals as well as literati-style gardens with a great number of standing strange-shaped sandstones with holes. Peter and I, with our guide and three women from three countries, took a high-speed train forty minutes westward from Shanghai to Suzhou, where a microbus was waiting to take us to the site.

A small temple compound is packed with Qin Dynasty buildings—the front gate, Buddha hall, Avalokiteshvara hall, dharma hall, guest hall, and bell hall. Beside the temple compound gracefully stands a large five-story circular pagoda. Some of these buildings, containing aged ochre and deep red walls with archaic slate roofs, survived the Cultural Revolution because they were used as cells for questioning prisoners, although most Buddhist images and ritual items were destroyed. The abbot at that time, Xingkong, had posted Chairman Mao's sayings all over the outside of the buildings so that a number of Hanshan and Shide tablets engraved on the outside walls were preserved.

According to *Wujun Zhi* (Record of Wu Country), this temple was founded during the Tianjian Era (502–519) of the southern kingdom of Liang as Miaoli Puming Pagoda Temple. There is a legend that in the Tang Dynasty, Hanshan built a hut and lived there before moving to Tiantai. Later Shitou Xiqian (700–790), as abbot, restored its desolate buildings and renamed it Hanshan Temple. Shitou—ordained by and eventually a second-generation dharma successor of the Sixth Chinese Ancestor, Huineng—is the author of the widely chanted Zen poems "Cantong Qi" (Being One and Many) and "Cao'an Ge" (Song of the Grass Hut).

Later, during the time of the An Lushan revolt (755–763) the poet Zhang Ji (d. 779) wrote a poem while passing by:

> Moon descends, crows cry, frost fills the sky.
> River maples—fishing torches—join my melancholy sleep.
> A Suzhou maiden stands outside the Hanshan Temple.
> The bell's midnight sound reaches the ferry.

This poem, according to the temple history, attained a "thousand-year-long fame" and made the temple widely known. As if to multiply this praise, over fifty carved stone tablets of the rendering of this poem by different calligraphers, including contemporary ones, are displayed in the hallways of the temple buildings. Previously, I have seen some calligraphic prints of this poem, some of which accompany paintings of Hanshan and Shide. This poem, a favorite theme of Japanese calligraphers as well, seems to be a source of an everlasting fervor around this temple.

Hanshan and Shide also occupy the sanctuary: there is the remains of a small stone square with a pillar saying, "Hanshan Well." Multiple black tablets with dual portraits and Hanshan poems are inlaid on the outside walls of main buildings, including the Buddha Hall.

On a poster-like mural of a building, an inscription beneath the colorful images of our two poets says, "Hanshan Temple is an ancestral garden of the harmonious culture." And in the Hanshan and Shide Hall, large golden statues of these two individuals are enshrined. Visitors offer incense, kneel, and bow. In shock, Peter said, "Look. These people are praying to the poets. I don't want anyone to pray to me, or I might be in the wrong profession!"

Mystery, Mystery . . .

There are so many things unknown about the poet: What were the approximate dates of his life? Where was he born? What were his family and given names? What was his background and education? What did he do for a living in his earlier life?

There is no mention of Hanshan in any texts of his time. So, Iritani and Matsumura say, "There is no proof at all to determine there was a personality called Hanshan." If it is genuine, the undated Record by Luqiu Yin represents the only exception to the lack of a record from Hanshan's time. Therefore, it is nearly impossible to determine the poet's dates.

According to *Xianchuan Shiyi* (Additions to Biographies of Sorcerers), compiled by the Daoist Du Guangting (859–933), Hanshan was in retreat on Mount Cuiping, Tiantai, around the Dali Era (776–779); he disappeared for some years and reappeared to the Daoist Li He in the twelfth year of Xiantong (871).[17]

A description written in 1189 states that Fenggan, a Zen monk associated with Hanshan, lived in the Guoqing Monastery, which Hanshan often visited, in the early years of the Zhenguan Era (627–649) of Tang.[18] In *Song Gaoseng Cuan* (Song Biography of High Monks), compiled in 988, there is a statement that Guishan Lingyou (771–853), cofounder of the Guiyang School, went up to Mount Tiantai and met Hanshan during the Yuanhe Era (806–821).[19] Also, according to the *Tiantaishan Guoqin Chansi Sanyin Jiji* (Collected Works of the Three Hermits at Guoqing Monastery, Mount Tiantai, compiled by Zhinan in 1189) and the *Guzunsu Yulu* (Recorded Sayings of Ancient Revered Masters: published in 1617), Zhaozhou (778–897), many of whose words would be studied as koans by later generations, met Hanshan and exchanged words with him.[20]

Besides, if we believe in the legend at Suzhou's Hanshan Temple, Hanshan was there some time before the death of Shitou in 790.

These accounts, recorded long after Hanshan's period, seem to point us to contrasting dates of his life that range from the early seventh century to the eighth or ninth century.

As Iriya notes, another clue for dating Hanshan is his use of Zen Buddhist terms such as "mind that is king," "dharma king," "true buddha," and "person beyond doing." These terms became commonly used after the Southern School of Zen, under the influence of the Sixth Chinese Ancestor, Dajian Huineng (638–713), started to flourish in the late seventh to early eighth century.[21]

As the name and title of the author of "Hanshan Shiji Xu" (Record of the Hanshan Anthology) is not found in any official record of the Tang Dynasty (618–907), the authenticity of this text has been questioned from the beginning in twentieth-century scholarship in Japan.[22] One scholar guessed that the entire collection of the Hanshan poems was a creation of Daoqiao, the Buddhist monk mentioned as the assembler of the poems according to the Record.[23]

Another verifiable instance of Hanshan being mentioned in a text seems to be *Linjian Lu* (Collection from Ancestral Halls), edited in 952.[24] So the poet's dates cannot be later than that, or the time of Du Guangting

(859–933) as mentioned above. Thus, a rough guess can be made that the poet lived somewhere between 730 and 933.[25]

Then, how do we know about the poet's life? Burton Watson suggests: "If the reader wishes to know the biography of Hanshan, he must deduce it from the poems themselves."[26] This is what Red Pine has done. He attempted to reconstruct Hanshan's life from scattered descriptions of events that seem to suggest his life.

According to conjectures by Red Pine, Hanshan was born in the ancient town of Hantan to a well-off, privileged family.[27] He recalls his early years in the capital city of Chang'an.[28] He takes us inside the imperial palace there.[29] He recalls hunting on horseback on a royal hill.[30] He had a bad leg.[31] With education he might have been an assistant to a high official; his employer was apparently in charge of taxation or conscription.[32] At one point he was married, but he left his family.[33] He witnessed the An Lushan rebellion of 755 to 757 that occupied the ancient capital of Luoyang.[34] Hanshan did leave home, usually meaning that he became a Buddhist monk.[35] He moved to Cold Mountain at age thirty.[36]

I applaud Red Pine for his meticulous endeavor to sketch out Hanshan's life. Our colleague seems to have made a maximum potential list of lines that may give clues about the poet's life. But the majority of the poems Red Pine has cited are descriptions of third-person males or females. It is debatable, therefore, that we should see all of them as Hanshan's autobiographical reflections.

There are poems, however, that use the words "I" or "my" in Chinese. One is poem 151 ("My original home is on Tiantai.") and others are poems 27 and 202 ("I live in a village").

On the other hand, Chinese sentences often imply the subjects or objects, and the reader or translator needs to imagine them. In this regard, poems that seem to imply the first person are poem 24 ("even my own wife turned her back. So I left the dusty world."), poem 102 ("Born thirty years ago, I've wandered thousands of miles"), poem 79 ("In last night's dream I returned home and saw my wife weaving"), poem 188 ("When I think back on places I came across in the past"), poem 233 ("Since leaving home I finally understand"), and poem 278 ("Thinking back over twenty years, I slowly walk to Guoqing Monastery"). But it is also possible to translate these poems into a third-person format, such as "even his wife turned her back. So he left."

Poem 30 says, "What a pity! Within a hundred years the capital city of Xian was destroyed." Xian is an ancient city, and its name also means Chang'an. Red Pine's suggestion to match this reference to the destruction of a city by the An Lushan revolt is fair. But the time span from the founding of the Tang Dynasty to the beginning of the revolt is 137 years, and not "within a hundred years." How do we resolve this discrepancy?

At this point, I have further questions about Hanshan's life and poetry:

> Was Hanshan as eccentric as portrayed?
> Is the "Record of the Hanshan Anthology" authentic?
> Why does the poet seem to have a diverse background, including Daoism and Buddhism?
> Why does he express contradictory views?
> Are there any other characteristics in his poetic style that can help determine the time period(s) of his writing?

Witness Examination

"Eccentric" is the default term that has been applied to the words and deeds of Hanshan in nearly all biographical descriptions of him for over one thousand years in China, Korea, Japan, and recently in the Western world.

All the Hanshan and Shide legends and artistic depictions seem to have come from a single source—"Hanshan Shiji Xu" (Record of the Hanshan Anthology). We are attaching a full translation of it preceding this essay. The author of the Record calls himself Luqiu Yin, governor of Tai Region. In this text he describes his encounter with Zen Master Fenggan, who suggests that he go to the Guoqing Monastery on Mount Tiantai and meet with Hanshan, who is Manjushri, a bodhisattva of wisdom reincarnated, and his comrade Shide, who is no other than Samantabhadra, the bodhisattva of practice. Yin then records his encounter with Hanshan and Shide, who laughed aloud, yelled at him, ran away, and disappeared. Later, Yin asks a Buddhist monk named Daoqiao to collect scattered poems by Hanshan. Thus, Luqiu Yin has been widely regarded as the one who compiled and introduced the Hanshan anthology.

If you read Hanshan's poems beyond the confinement of the myth of absurdity, you may find Hanshan to be a sincere seeker of truth, a clear observer of affairs in life, and an honest speaker. As a hermit, he must have avoided social occasions, but he longed for a chance to speak with seekers of the way, and perhaps did not want to miss the opportunity to give advice to people who were willing to listen.

Certainly there was an element of eccentricity in his poems. For example, he wrote about himself as speaking like a confused madman or being viewed as crazy.[37] Besides, as I suggested earlier, he was ill dressed.[38] His lifestyle was not usual, and his values were beyond the comprehension of many of those who were busy making their living or seeking success in society. One poem relates a fantasy about sleeping on a tiger-head pillow.[39] These poems and anecdotes can be the basis of the Hanshan legend. However, laughing, yelling, and running away, described in the Record by Luqiu Yin, who was the presumed solo witness of the poet, seem to be an overstated characterization of the poet.

An examination of the accounts in the Record poses a number of questions. Some of the descriptions seem not only bizarre but unrealistic: "Nobody is at Fenggan's temple except for a tiger, who is often there and roars"; "Hanshan and Shide held each other's hand and ran out of the monastery"; "Hanshan saw the messenger and yelled out, 'Thief, thief!'"; "The opening of the cave closed itself"; "He had written [poems] on bamboo, wood, stones, walls of village houses and offices." Also, identifying these hermits as the bodhisattvas Manjushri and Samanthabhadra—Buddhist deities, so to speak, often enshrined on altars—reveals a mythological aspect of the Record. The text thus appears to be a product of imagination by someone who had never visited the actual sites.

In terms of the date of this Record, Iriya noted without giving specific reasons: "I do not accept it as something so old. I think it is a forgery of the ninth to tenth century."[40] This may be just a presumption, but it is reasonable to see the Record as having been written when the Hanshan legend had developed some time after his death. Certainly, Iriya's statement liberates us from the traditional notion that Luqiu Yin was a genuine witness of Hanshan and Shide and that he was responsible for the compilation of the Hanshan anthology.

In fact, we need to deconstruct the narrative of the fictional Record and disregard images of the established genre of Hanshan and Shide paintings. Thus, we set the Hanshan poems free from the spell of the myth of the poet's strange personality. By doing so, we come to see the poems as they are without branding them as eccentric.

Critical Views of the Poet

Hanshan's poems imply that he had a varied background in his early life: a farmer, trader, scholar, family man, hermit, Daoist, and Buddhist. He often despises and criticizes people who look for material gain, yet he gives advice to people to be wise about financial management. This makes us wonder if the Hanshan poems were written by more than one person.

Seitan Shaku says in his book *Kanzan Shi Shinshaku* (New Interpretation of the Hanshan Poems), published in 1907, "There are two Hanshans. One is genuine and the other is false. Only after separating these two should we speak of Hanshan."[41]

Later, the Japanese historian Sokichi Tsuda (1873–1961) had observed evidence that along with the development of Hanshan folklore, some poems that support it were added.[42] Iriya also says, "It is difficult to limit the authorship of this anthology to a single person."[43] His statement is echoed by Iritani and Matsumura: "At present there is no other way of saying that we should call the writers of the group of poems included in the 'Hanshan Anthology' Hanshan."

Iritani and Matsumura also suggest that the Hanshan poems were highly influenced by a textbook of poetry called *Wen Xuan* (Selected Literature), edited by Xiaotong (501–531) of the Liang Dynasty, which was widely used for people who applied for the examination taken by those who hoped to become government officials. They also point out that the Hanshan poems have many references to ancient literature and history books.[44] Not only that, they say that the Hanshan poems have phrases that correspond to those by Li Bo (701–762) and Du Fu (712–770). In this regard, they say, "Unless there is evidence that the Hanshan poems were widely read by poets of the prime and middle time Tang poets like Li Bo and Du Fu, it should be natural that Hanshan borrowed poetic words from these great poets."[45]

Burton Watson, who acknowledges Iriya's contribution to his translation, also suggests: "Though some of the poems in the collection are probably later additions, a large part of them appears to be by one man."[46]

In regard to Watson's suggestion, E. G. Pulleyblank, a prominent Canadian expert in Chinese study, presents in 1977 a stunning theory in his paper titled "Linguistic Evidence for the Date of Hanshan." He suggests: "Happily a study of the rhymes gives objective support to this conclusion and (within limits . . .) helps one to separate the works of the original poet from the later accretions."[47]

Meter and Rhyme

Before introducing the Pulleyblank theory, let me summarize a common poetic form of Chinese classical verse, including Hanshan's.

The majority of the Hanshan poems have a meter represented by five ideographs per column. (Columns run from right to left.) They are presented in our book in the form of five ideographs per *line*, as we have made each vertical column into a horizontal line to go with our English translation. Other Hanshan poems are in the format of seven or three ideographs per column.

In the Chinese language, each ideograph is pronounced as a syllable and acts as a word. A syllable is either a vowel or a consonant (initial) followed by a "vowel" (a final sound that may end with such a subtle consonant as -*ng*).

The vowel or final of each syllable has one of the four tones: the first or upper even tone (i.e., ā), the second or rising tone (i.e., á), the third or lower-rising tone (i.e., ǎ), or the fourth or falling tone (i.e., à). The foot of a Hanshan poem rhymes on every other line. Let's take the first Hanshan poem, for example, which reads in modern Mandarin:[48]

> rén wèn hán shān dào
> hán shān lù bù tōng
> xià tiān bīng wèi shì
> rì chū wù méng lóng
> sì wǒ hé yóu jiè
> yǔ jūn xīn bù tóng
> jūn xīn ruò sì wǒ
> huán dé dào qí zhōng

> 人間寒山道
> 寒山路不通
> 夏天冰未釋
> 日出霧朦朧
> 似我何由屆
> 與君心不同
> 君心若似我
> 還得到其中

Here, the -*ōng* and -*óng* syllables at the end of the even-numbered columns (lines two, four, six, and eight) roughly rhyme in Mandarin, but they do so perfectly in the classical standard.[49]

Early examples of meter with the same or similar number of ideographs per column, and with rhyme on every or every other column, are already seen in the *Shi Jing* (Book of Odes), which includes more than three hundred songs from the eleventh to six centuries B.C.E.[50] In the Later Han

Dynasty (25–220), more samples of a meter of five ideographs per column and rhyming on even-numbered columns emerged, and this format became common in the second to third century during the Wei Dynasty. These types of poems flourished greatly during the Tang Dynasty and beyond, although there were some poems that also rhymed in irregular columns.

The classical standard dictionary of Chinese pronunciation, the *Qie Yun* (Essential Rhyming), published in 601, was followed by the *Guang Yun* (Extensive Rhyming), published in 1007. The latter lists 206 tonal syllable groups.[51] The Swedish linguist Klas Bernhard Johannes Karlgren (1889–1978) established lists of tonal syllables for Early Middle Chinese and Later Middle Chinese using the Western linguistic method.[52] The *Qie Yun* dates from the Sui Dynasty to the early Tang periods (the later sixth to early seventh century) and the *Guang Yun* to the later Tang period (the ninth to early tenth century). Pulleyblank published in 1991 the *Lexicon of Reconstructed Pronunciation: In Early Middle Chinese, Late Middle Chinese, and Early Mandarin*, which includes the pronunciation of approximately eight thousand ideographs.

According to Pulleyblank, the Early Middle Chinese differentiates the i̱ of *zhī* (脂) group from the i̱ of *zhī* (之) group as in International Phonetic Alphabet tɕi and tɕi, while they merge as tʂi in the Later Middle Chinese. Also, the Early Middle Chinese keeps the ē of *dēng* (登) group apart from the ē of *dēng* (蒸) group, as well as the ú of *yú* (魚) group from the ú of *yú* (虞) group, for example, whereas these tonal syllables were merged in Later Middle Chinese.[53] The majority of the Hanshan poems strictly observe rhyming in the Early Middle Chinese.

Pulleyblank classifies the poems rhymed in the manner of Early Middle Chinese as "Hanshan I" and those that fit into Later Middle Chinese as "Hanshan II." He then suggests that "while a portion of the poems must clearly be of the late Tang date, another considerably larger portion shows rhyming which points very strongly to the early Tang or Sui dates."[54] He concludes that most of the vibrant Hanshan poems belong to Hanshan I and that some of the Hanshan II poems read like dry "didactic sermons."[55]

He also notes that all poems attributed to Shide have all the characteristics of late Tang rhyming and in addition some further mergers of tonal syllables that can be dated from the Northern Song (960–1126).[56] (Because Pulleyblank's presentation is very technical, I have taken the liberty of paraphrasing his discussion with some additional information for the reader.)

Henricks suggests that Pulleyblank's analysis of rhymes in the Hanshan poems is the most important contribution in Hanshan scholarship to date in determining the timeline of the poet (or poets). Commenting that "the linguistic evidence is persuasive, and I think most literary scholars these days assume the truth of this thesis as a working position; it is certainly possible that counter-theses will be argued later on,"[57] Henricks adopts Pulleyblank's theory and distinguishes a Hanshan II poem with an asterisk after the number of some of his translated poems. After examining the rhyming of all the Hanshan poems Pulleyblank analyzed, I fully agree with Henricks on his evaluation of Pulleyblank's remarkable breakthrough in Hanshan studies.

Thus, Pulleyblank's scholarship leads us to presume that the Hanshan poems were written in two periods, which pushes the date of the original poet, Hanshan, back to the Sui Dynasty (581–618) or an early part of the Tang Dynasty (618–907). This means his dates are likely in the late sixth to early seventh century. In contrast, the later addition can be placed in the ninth century.

Hanshan I poems were written before the influence of Zen expanded in China. Then, after Zen spread widely throughout the country, it is possible that some later poet(s) attempted to pull Hanshan to his (their) Zen camp. The legends that Zen masters Zhauzhou and Guishan met Hanshan seem to have developed as part of this trend.

Pulleyblank rightly cautions: "One cannot, unfortunately, determine with certainty solely on the basis of rhymes alone which poems came from each layer."

Red Pine argues: "Pulleyblank, however, overlooks the fact that such Hanshan I poems as [RP] 113, 119, and 178 refer to events of the eighth century. While linguistic analysis may work in a perfect world, it fails here. I suggest, instead, that Cold Mountain, like most Chinese today, spoke at least two dialects, one of which was more archaic than the other(s) and that this is reflected in his poems."[58]

Henricks echoes Red Pine in this regard: "I still remain troubled by poems like [H] 120 and 179, which are by rhyme words Hanshan I poems and which in style and theme correspond to that group, but which seem to contain—clearly in the case of 120—references to things in mid-Tang (c. 750 AD)."[59] This poses a question: who wrote poems with Early Middle Chinese rhyming that include references to words or matters that only existed in the later period?

Three Hanshan Poets

In addition to Henricks's concern, as just mentioned, I feel other poems in the Hanshan I group seem to have words that have later Zen references: "A mosquito biting an iron ox," "recognize the king of dharma," "priceless treasure in the mind," "those who don't know letters," "returning to your original mind is itself buddha," and "original person."[60]

Then, how can we explain that some of the Hanshan I poems with Early Middle Chinese rhyming have reference to expressions or matters from later times—namely, the mid-Tang period? Is it not possible to presume that these poems were written later with faithful copying of the original Hanshan's Early Middle Chinese rhyming? If so, these poems can be regarded as an early addition to Hanshan I and as belonging to a group that may be placed between Hanshan I and Hanshan II poems.

Now that we have isolated some clear cases of the later poems from the Hanshan I group, we have a choice about how to deal with the rest of the poems in this group. One: keep the rest of the Hanshan I poems as they are, assuming the original poet Hanshan was a Daoist as well as a Buddhist, or a Daoist who converted to Buddhism. Two: move all the Buddhist and Zen-related poems to the middle group, keeping the Daoist Hanshan as author of the original Hanshan I poems, and placing the Buddhist poet Hanshan's works in the category of an early addition to the original Hanshan poems—a group I suggest be newly created.

The second choice makes more sense to me. Being a hermit is a serious commitment; it seems to me more plausible that the original Hanshan was a dedicated or fully inclined Daoist rather than a practitioner of a mixture of the two paths, or that he became more inclined to Buddhism right before or after he entered Cold Mountain.

Either way, we see at least three Hanshan poets responsible for creating the Hanshan anthology: the original one, the one who followed his rhymes and wrote Zen-influenced and possibly general Buddhist-themed poems, and a further later poet who wrote Hanshan II poems in Late Middle Chinese rhyming.

The original poet Hanshan lived on Mount Tiantai in southern China, but Pulleyblank suggests that there are linguistic reasons for thinking that he probably originated from the north, such as the capital city of Luoyang or Chang'an.[61] This poet wrote in Early Middle Chinese rhyming, which was used during the Sui Dynasty (589–617) or an early part of the Tang Dynasty (618–907). Pulleyblank also suggests: "Since Hanshan is clearly a rustic poet, this can only be because the distinctions he followed [in rhyming] were part of his actual speech, not learned from a dictionary." Thus, in all likelihood, the original Hanshan lived in the late sixth to early seventh century, before Zen was widely practiced. He was a Daoist practitioner, and whether he later was influenced by Buddhism requires a further debate.

(As the original Hanshan dates have been determined, there can be a new understanding of poem 30 [RP 178], which Red Pine intended to match with the An Lushan revolt and destruction of Luoyang. The poem may, instead, describe the destruction of Chang'an due to the farmers' revolt at the end of the Sui Dynasty and the civil war before the establishment of the Tang Dynasty.)

The second Hanshan poet was certainly a Buddhist under considerable influence from the newly spreading Zen School. He possibly lived in the eighth or ninth century during the Later Middle Chinese language period. But he studied the original Hanshan's rhyming, possibly with a dictionary, and closely followed the original Hanshan's poetic form.

The third Hanshan possibly lived later than the second Hanshan. He followed the rhyming of his own time—Later Middle Chinese—and composed additional Hanshan poems. He wrote in the style of the original Hanshan with the projection that this Hanshan was a Zen practitioner, resulting in making the original Hanshan a hero among Zen practitioners.

In this way, I suggest that there were at least three Hanshan poets. Traditionally, however, Hanshan was regarded as one poet, and you may still see just one. A similar yet contrary example is the Buddha. When a dharma teacher suggests, "The Buddha says . . .," we need to ask, "In which sutra?" There are a great number of Buddhist scriptures that emerged throughout the centuries that quote him, but we have no problem seeing the Buddha as one person. In contrast, Hanshan has only one source, the anthology, which was possibly contributed to by at least three poets. Would it be acceptable likewise to see Hanshan as one poet with three bodies from different times?

Text and Our Presentation of the Poems

Our base text for the translation is the oldest and most comprehensive version of the Hanshan anthology—the Song Dynasty version, which was originally called *Tiantaishan Guoqin Chansi Sanyin Jiji* (Collected Works of the Three Hermits Collection at the Guoqing Monastery, Mount Tiantai), compiled by Zhinan in 1189, with a later postscript by Huashan Keming in 1229. This version is known in Japan as the Imperial Household Library Version. It is published as *Kanzan Shi* (Hanshan Poems) by Teizo Ota and later translated by Robert G. Henricks. Ota's version contains Luqiu Yin's Record and 312 Hanshan poems. It also includes two Fenggan poems and fifty-six Shide poems, which came from the Hanshan anthology included in the *Quan Tang Shi* (Entire Tang Poems), and later published in Japan in 1647. We present a translation of Luqiu Yin's Record on pages 211–15 but do not include the Fenggan and Shide poems.

We add one Hanshan poem cited earlier than the Song Dynasty version. That is poem 291. It was quoted by Zen Master Huihong Juefan (1071–1128) as his favorite poem in his *Linjian Lu* (Collection of Ancestral Halls) published in 1107.

Following the findings by Edwin G. Pulleyblank, mentioned above in and after the section "Critical Views of the Poet," and my own hypothesis about three Hanshan poets, we present the poems in three parts: original poems, early additions, and later additions—all presumed.

In part one, to open our edition, we first present five poems similar to traditional versions that include Hanshan's description of his hermitic experience. Then we follow the grouping of poems used by Watson, who says, "Since they seem from the beginning to have had no fixed order, I have taken the liberty of making my own arrangement in the translation:

- Poems that clearly deal with the poet's early life, along with some conventional romantic lyrics.
- Satires and poems showing the writer's increasing disgust with the world, many of them marked by considerable spleen and self-pity.
- Poems on his retirement to Cold Mountain, his experiences there, and the alternating modes of elation and despair which beset him.[62]

The last group in Watson's classification—a group of poems on Buddhist themes—are placed in parts two or three.

As mentioned above, we have concrete reasons to believe the existence of at least three Hanshan poets. First of all, it is clear that all poems in Late Middle Chinese rhyming should be placed in part three. However, the division between poems in parts one and two are a working proposition. All poems in Early Middle Chinese rhyming with Buddhist themes or terminology are placed in part two. This may be a subject for future debate. Also you will find poems in the early rhyming that have references to mid-seventh-to-eighth-century phrases or events in part two; in those cases we try to explain, in notes to the poems, why they are placed in part two. Our intention is to offer the reader an opportunity to view the Hanshan poems from the perspective of the most advanced and still evolving scholarship.

Notes

1. *Kanzan Shi Sendai Kimon*, completed during the Enkyo Era (1744–1748).
2. Hakuin wrote this commentary in Chinese, solely with ideographs, different from his usual way of writing in Japanese, which is a mixture of ideographs and phonetics. In Chinese an ideograph functions as a word.
3. Hakuin, *Hakuin Osho Zenshu*, vol. 4, 31. Commenting on poem 3.
4. Ibid., 47. Commenting on poem 104.
5. Ibid. Commenting on poem 13.
6. Three other Edo Period commentaries are *Shusho Kanzan Shi* (Headnotes, Hanshan Poems), commentator unknown, three fascicles, Kambun Era (1661–1673); *Kanzan Shi Gange* (Commentary on Hanshan Poems) by Koi, six fascicles, Genroku Era (1688–1704); *Kanzan Shi Sakui* (Exploring Clues to Hanshan Poems), by Daitei, three fascicles, Bunka Era (1804–1818). Ota, 8. Kusumoto, 31.
7. Ota, 4.
8. Ota, 5.
9. Hakuin, *Hakuin Osho Zenshu*, vol. 4, 27.
10. Notably, Fujita Museum, Osaka: one panel by Liangkai, twelfth to thirteenth century, China. Tokyo National Museum: one panel by Yintuoluo, fourteenth century, China; one panel attributed to Shubun (1782–1861), Japan.
11. The Japanese have developed a systematized way of reading Chinese by adding phonetics in between the original ideographs, and sometimes reversing the reading sequences. This is called *kambun yomi* (Japanese way of reading Chinese text).
12. Iriya, Yoshitaka, *Kanzan*.
13. Waley, *Encounter*, 3:3, September 1954. Quoted by Watson, 10.
14. Kerouac, J., *The Dharma Bums* (New York: The Viking Press, 1985; republished, New York: Penguin Books, 1976), 22.
15. Poem 233.
16. Red Pine says, "It's actually more of a huge overhang than a cave. Roughly sixty meters across, thirty meters deep and ten meters high." Red Pine, 4.
17. This description was quoted in *Taiping Guangji* (Extensive Record of Peaceful Time), a collection of tales compiled in Song Dynasty, five hundred fascicles.
18. Henricks, 4.
19. *Song Gaoseng Zhuan*, fascicle 11. Ota, 4.

20. *Tiantaishan Guoqin Chansi Sanyin Jiji*, also *Guzunsu Yulu*, fascicle 14. Iriya, 8.

21. Iriya, 16, "mind that is king," poem 305; "dharma king," poems 268 and 299; "true buddha," poem 268; and "person beyond doing," poems 277 and 251.

22. Ota, 3.

23. Ota, 4.

24. Iriya, 9.

25. Later in this essay I will present further considerations on Hanshan's dates.

26. Watson, 9.

27. Red Pine, 13, poems RP 27 and RP 47, poem RP 176, poem RP 21.

28. Ibid., poem RP 178.

29. Ibid., poems RP 19, RP 20, RP 39, and RP 48.

30. Ibid., poem RP 104.

31. Ibid., poems RP 25, RP 49, RP 71, RP 81, RP 113, RP 259, and RP 271.

32. Ibid., poems RP 51, RP 57, RP 63, RP 64, RP 65, and RP 81.

33. Ibid., 14, poems RP 21, RP 31, RP 134, RP 137, and RP 111.

34. Ibid., poem RP 178.

35. Ibid., poem RP 267.

36. Ibid., poem RP 131.

37. Henricks, 8, poems 280 and 314.

38. Poem 27.

39. Poem 201.

40. Iriya, 9.

41. Shaku, 4.

42. Iriya, 12; Tsuda, 148.

43. Iriya, 12.

44. We will explain Hanshan's references to earlier texts in our notes to his poems as much as possible, but we will not comprehensively show sources of poetic phrases. The reader may find such thorough scholarship in the book by Henricks.

45. Iritani and Matsumura, 490.

46. Watson, 9.

47. Henriks, 6; Edwin G. Pulleyblank, "Linguistic Evidence for the Date of Han-shan."

48. Poem H 1.

49. Here in my essay, I displayed the modern Mandarin transliteration. But even in present-day China, poets are required to consult with *Guang Yun* (Extensive Rhyming), compiled in 1007, to make their rhyming traditionally proper. The four characters I am showing as an example were pronounced in Early Middle Chinese, according to Edwin G. Pulleyblank's *Lexicon of Reconstructed Pronunciation* (Vancouver: UBC Books, 1991), using International Phonetic Alphabet: t^həwŋ, luawŋ, dəwŋ, and truwŋ. Thus, they rhyme according to traditional standards.

50. In this book, poems with four ideographs per column are more common.

51. Kadokawa, *Kan'wa Shin Jigen* (Kadokawa's New Chinese Japanese Ideograph Sources), 1184.

52. Ibid.

53. Further, Pulleyblank suggests that as opposed to the merging of the following similar tonal syllables in Later Middle Chinese, Hanshan, as in Early Middle Chinese, differentiates tán (覃) group from tán (談) group; hén (痕) group from hún (魂) group; āo (坳) group from hóu (侯) group; qēng (庚 and 耕) groups from qīng (清) group; xiāo (蕭) group from xiāo (宵) group; and qí (齊) group from jì (祭) group. Pulleyblank, 170–2.

54. Ibid, 164.

55. Ibid, 174.

56. Ibid, 174–5.

57. Henricks, 6.

58. Red Pine, 15.

59. Henricks, 7. His note on poem H120: the Southern Court was "established in 734 in the Bureau of Appointments of the Ministry of Personnel," Henricks, 182.

60. Poems 156 (Yaoshan's word), 167, 190, 195, 204, and 220.

61. Pulleyblank, 165.

62. Watson, 12.

Comparative List of Poem Numbers

The list below compares the poem numbers in this translation with the translations by Red Pine (RP) and Robert G. Henricks (H).

OURS	RP	H	OURS	RP	H	OURS	RP	H
1	16	9	21	64	61	41	17	10
2	32	28	22	75	73	42	15	8
3	1	2	23	101	101	43	18	11
4	4	20	24	111	111	44	23	17
5	3	3	25	140	137	45	36	32
6	12	5	26	113	113	46	38	34
7	5	51	27	220	222	47	40	36
8	180	181	28	121	122	48	41	37
9	19	12	29	173	174	49	42	38
10	7	14	30	178	179	50	43	39
11	8	21	31	289	292	51	46	42
12	20	13	32	65	62	52	50	46
13	21	15	33	242	26	53	52	48
14	28	23	34	73	71	54	55	52
15	31	27	35	104	104	55	56	53
16	222	224	36	47	43	56	58	55
17	39	35	37	108	108	57	294	298
18	51	47	38	49	45	58	61	58
19	63	60	39	13	6	59	62	59
20	54	50	40	14	7	60	69	66

OURS	RP	H	OURS	RP	H	OURS	RP	H
61	80	79	93	216	218	125	150	147
62	153	150	94	227	229	126	33	29
63	239	242	95	283	286	127	172	173
64	93	93	96	276	279	128	278	281
65	99	99	97	94	94	129	81	80
66	110	110	98	270	273	130	34	30
67	114	114	99	87	86	131	70	68
68	115	115	100	67	64	132	133	130
69	120	116	101	9	295	133	6	67
70	116	117	102	131	300	134	147	144
71	123	124	103	79	78	135	37	33
72	124	125	104	22	16	136	301	305
73	125	126	105	219	221	137	24	18
74	126	127	106	83	82	138	48	44
75	127	128	107	193	193	139	71	69
76	128	129	108	194	199	140	303	307
77	135	132	109	107	107	141	287	290
78	136	133	110	144	141	142	25	19
79	137	134	111	268	270	143	166	166
80	138	135	112	102	102	144		211
81	143	140	113	197	190	145	304	308
82	146	143	114	174	175	146	2	1
83	148	145	115	285	288	147	158	155
84	149	146	116	30	25	148	11	4
85	161	158	117	27	22	149	44	40
86	154	151	118	261	262	150	259	260
87	156	153	119	263	265	151	207	205
88	152	149	120	191	194	152	10	277
89	151	148	121	175	176	153	45	41
90	198	191	122	157	154	154	53	49
91	221	223	123	29	24	155	57	54
92	252	253	124	35	35	156	66	63

OURS	RP	H	OURS	RP	H	OURS	RP	H
157	68	65	189	183	184	221	280	283
158	88	87	190	185	195	222	282	285
159	85	84	191	187	197	223	288	291
160	72	70	192	189	187	224	295	77
161	74	72	193	190	188	225	297	301
162	76	74	194	200	206	226	299	303
163	77	75	195	201	207	227		91
164	78	76	196	202	208	228		198
165	89	88	197	203	201	229	165	165
166	90	89	198	205	203	230	307	311
167	91	90	199	206	204	231	226	228
168	92	92	200	208	209	232	118	119
169	95	95	201	182	183	233	267	269
170	184	185	202	284	287	234	237	240
171	96	96	203	209	210	235	292	296
172	298	302	204	210	212	236	82	81
173	100	100	205	217	219	237	204	202
174	105	105	206	223	225	238	192	192
175	112	112	207	224	226	239	134	131
176	117	118	208	229	231	240	106	106
177	119	120	209	232	234	241	26	163
178	122	123	210	233	235	242	163	161
179	130	299	211	240	243	243	279	282
180	139	136	212	250	251	244	255	256
181	141	138	213	266	268	245		263
182	142	139	214	251	252	246	169	170
183	145	142	215	253	254	247	302	306
184	155	152	216	269	271	248	274	276
185	159	156	217	256	257	249		
186	160	157	218	258	259	250	244	244
187	170	171	219	264	266	251	245	246
188	176	177	220	275	278	252	291	294

OURS	RP	H	OURS	RP	H	OURS	RP	H
253	265	267	275	179	180	297	247	248
254		164	276	230	232	298	132	167
255	290	293	277	231	233	299	241	159A
256	213	215	278	271	274	300	199	200
257	181	182	279	86	85	301	243	244
258	262	264	280	234	236	302	272	275A
259	254	255	281	98	98	303	273	275B
260	306	310	282	188	186	304		237
261	277	280	283	211	213	305	281	284
262	215	217	284	109	109	306	260	261
263	249	250	285	167	168	307	286	289
264	246	247	286	103	103	308	296	121
265	196	189	287	97	97	309	195	196
266	236	239	288	238	241		186	
267	171	172	289	59	56	310	300	304
268	214	216	290	60	57	311	84	83
269	177	178	291			312	293	297
270	168	169	292	235	238	313	241B	159B
271	228	230	293	129	272	314	218	220
272	225	227	294	257	258	315	305	309
273	164	162	295	248	249			
274	162	160	296	212	214			

Acknowledgments

First, we would like to thank Dr. Edwin G. Pulleyblank for his outstanding study of the rhyming patterns in Hanshan's poems, which revealed that there were at least two Hanshan poets. His work formed the basis for our conclusion that there were at least three Hanshan poets. The translated poems of Hanshan by Gary Snyder and Burton Watson have inspired us for half a century, and we have benefited greatly from the scholarship of Prof. Robert G. Henricks and Red Pine.

While exploring the inner meanings of Hanshan's poems, we often referred to works by Prof. Bun'yu Kusumoto, as well as those of Dr. Sensuke Iritani and Dr. Takashi Matsumura. Commentaries by Zen Master Hakuin, Rev. Seitan Shaku, Dr. Sokichi Tsuda, Teizo Ota, Yoshitaka Iriya, Dr. Keiji Nishitani, and Daisen Nobuhara have also been sources of our study. We thank Rev. Senkan Hongo for the use of a reproduction of the Hanshan and Shide painting by Sansetsu Kano. Our gratitude goes to Dr. Susan O'Leary, Dr. Szevone Chin, and Rev. Roberta Werdinger for their valuable editorial advice. Thanks also to Yuka Saito and Shoma Murakawa for their help.

We thank Roshi Joan Halifax and the staff of the Upaya Zen Center for helping to organize our Dogen and Hanshan pilgrimage in China. Our appreciation goes to Eric Lu for his excellent guiding on the pilgrimage. We thank Victoria Shoemaker and Anne Edelstein for representing us.

We offer gratitude to our spouses, Dr. Linda Hess and Dr. Shirley Graham, for their continuous, loving support and delightful hospitality. Linda answered all of Kaz's questions about the English language, and Shirley gave her insightful responses as Peter read her many of the poems. Translating Hanshan's poems together has been an extremely enjoyable experience for both of us.

It's been a great pleasure to work with our friends at Shambhala Publications, including Hazel Bercholz and Nikko Odiseos. We thank John Golebiewski for his excellent editing and Dave O'Neal, who has guided us from the conception of the book throughout its production.

KAZUAKI TANAHASHI *and* PETER LEVITT

Bibliography

English

Henricks, Robert G. *The Poetry of Han-shan: A Complete, Annotated Translation of* "Cold Mountain." Albany: State University of New York Press, 1990.

Pulleyblank, Edwin G. "Linguistic Evidence for the Date of Han-shan." In Ronald C. Miao, ed., *Studies in Chinese Poetry and Politics*, vol. 1. San Francisco: CMC, 1978.

Red Pine, tr. *The Collected Songs of Cold Mountain.* Port Townsend, WA: Copper Canyon Press, 1983.

Rouzer, Paul, tr. *The Poetry of Hanshan (Cold Mountain), Shide, and Fenggan.* Boston: Walter de Gruyter, 2017.

Snyder, Gary, tr. "Cold Mountain Poems." *Evergreen Review* 2 (Autumn 1958): 6. Reprinted in *Riprap and Cold Mountain Poems.* San Francisco: Four Seasons Foundation, 1965. New edition: Berkeley, CA: Counterpoint, 2013.

Waley, Arthur, tr. "27 Poems by Han-shan." *Encounter* 3 (September 1954): 3.

Watson, Burton, tr. *Cold Mountain: 100 Poems by the T'ang Poet Han-shan.* New York: Columbia University Press, 1970.

Japanese

Hakuin Ekaku. *Kanzan Shi Sendai Kimon* (Icchantica's Notes on the Hanshan Poems), completed during the Enkyo Era (1744–1748), *Hakuin Oshō Zenshū* (The Complete Writings of the Priest Hakuin), vol. 4. Tokyo: Ryugin Sha, 1934.

Iritani Sensuke and Matsumura Takashi, ed. *Kanzan Shi* (Hanshan Poems). Tokyo: Chikuma Shobo, 1958.

Iriya Yoshitaka. *Kanzan* (Hanshan). Tokyo: Iwanami Shoten, 1958.

Matsumura Takashi. *Furo de Yomu Kanzan Jittoku* (Hanshan and Shide Poems for Your Bath Time). Kyoto: Sekei Shiso Sha, 1996.

Nishitani Keiji. *Kanzan Shi* (Hanshan Poems). Tokyo: Chikuma Shobo, 1986.

Nobuhara Daisen. *Heiyaku Kanzan Shi* (Easy Translation: Hanshan Poems). Tokyo: Meitoku Shuppansha, 1961.

Ota Teizo. *Kanzan Shi* (Hanshan Poems). Tokyo: Iwanami Shoten, 1934.

Kusumoto Bun'yu. *Zayuban Kanzan Jittoku* (Entire Translation: Hanshan and Shide). Tokyo: Kodansha, 1995.

Shaku Seitan. *Kanzan Shi Shinshaku* (New Interpretation of the Hanshan Poems). Tokyo: Heigo Shuppansha, 1907.

Tsuda Sokichi. "Kanzan Jittoku Setsuwa ni tsui te." (On Hanshan and Shide Tales). *Tsuda Sokichi Zenshu* (Complete Works of Sokichi Tsuda), vol. 19. Tokyo: Iwanami Shoten, 1965.

Chinese

Wang Hainan and Zhang Alian. *Hanshan Si* (Hanshan Temple). Beijing: Zongjiao Wenhua Chubanshe, 2015.

Wen Bo. *Hanshan Shihua* (A Brief History of Hanshan Temple). Beijing: Social Sciences Academic Press, 2016.

Index of First Lines

About the Translators

KAZUAKI TANAHASHI, a Buddhist scholar, has translated the writings of Zen Masters Dogen, Hakuin, and Ryokan. He was born in Japan in 1933 and has been active in the United States since 1977. He is also a painter and calligrapher, as well as a peace activist.

PETER LEVITT has published books of poetry, prose, and translation, including the writings of Zen Master Dogen with Kazuaki Tanahashi. In 1989, he received the Lannan Foundation Award in Poetry. He is the guiding teacher of the Salt Spring Zen Circle on Salt Spring Island, British Columbia, where he lives with his wife, poet Shirley Graham, and their son, Tai.